CHAPTER ONE
THE ORIGINS OF THE MÉTI

C000042069

The municipal area of the city of Paris is still defi.
existed until the 1920s. The area immediately beyond the city formed ror many years....
Département of the Seine but has now been sub-divided into Seine-Saint-Denis, Hauts-de-Seine and Val-de-Marne. The area of greater Paris spreads even beyond this, into the Départements of Seine-et-Marne, Yvelines, Essonne and Val d'Oise. Together the city and these Départements form the region of Île-de-France and overall planning, including transport planning is the responsibility of the region.

The existence of the city walls had a psychological as well as a physical effect on the growth of the city and as late as the 1890s Paris had still not experienced the suburban sprawl which had become a feature of London. The central area had, however, been greatly enlarged and rebuilt during the Second Empire and among the improvements was the construction of a central produce market, Les Halles. The first proposal for an underground railway, to link Les Halles with the Gare du Nord and the Gare de Lyon, was made in 1856 and the idea was taken sufficiently seriously for the basement of Les Halles to be laid out to allow for its passage. Unfortunately, by the time a railway, in the shape of RER line A, actually reached the spot, the market itself had migrated to the suburbs.

The next forty years saw the publication of a plethora of plans for urban railways, many of which were marked more by their ingenuity than by their feasibility. Suspended monorail lines and a railway constructed in the middle of the Seine appeared alongside more conventional plans for elevated lines on the American model. The Law of 11 June 1880, allowing local communities to build railways of a local nature (chemins de fer d'intérêt local) ushered in a fifteen year conflict between the City of Paris, whose politicians wanted to build a purely urban system, and the national government, strongly supported by the main line railway companies, which would have preferred a system somewhat along the lines of today's RER and built to main line standards. The municipal plans tended to centre around what ultimately became lines 2, 3 and 6 of the Métro but the authorities also supported a plan for a tube line, to be worked by electricity, from Porte de Vincennes to Porte Dauphine. The sharp curves and steep gradients of this line made it the true precursor of the Métro, though it seems to have been seen more as a tramway than as a railway. When the author of this scheme, Jean-Baptiste Berlier, was unable to raise the necessary capital, the City added it to its own plans.

The arguments might have gone on indefinitely had not the approach of an international exhibition, planned for 1900, concentrated the official mind wonderfully. In 1896 the municipality decided to adopt a system of six lines, to be built to metre gauge, using carriages which would be only 1.9m wide. The system was to be worked by electric traction. When the concession was advertised, six tenders were received and it was awarded to the Compagnie Générale de Traction, part of a group headed by the Belgian financier the Baron Empain. The Compagnie d'Electricité de Paris also formed part of this group and the Métro was clearly seen as an important customer for the latter's product.

The agreement between the City and the CGT was signed in January 1898. The City would build the tunnels and the platforms of the stations while the CGT would be responsible for providing access to the stations, laying the track and buying the rolling stock. This agreement then went to the national government for ratification. The latter insisted that the track gauge should be the standard one of 1435mm and that the width of the carriages should be increased to 2.4m, though the loading gauge remained too narrow to permit the passage of main line trains. With these amendments agreed, the plan was authorised by the Law of 30 March 1898 and the CGT went on to form a limited company, the Compagnie de Chemin de Fer Métropolitan de Paris, normally and henceforth referred to as the CMP, to operate the system.

The concession was fixed for period of 35 years from the completion of the network outlined in the agreement. The City was to receive one third of the price of each second class ticket sold and 40% of each first class ticket, with a supplementary payment if the number of passengers rose above 140 million in any one year. These payments were intended to offset the loan which the City was to raise to finance the construction of the system. The figure of 140 million passengers was first reached in 1904.

By an inspired stroke, the City entrusted the building of the system to Fulgence Bienvenüe, an engineer of the Public Works Board for Roads and Bridges. Bienvenüe had considerable experience of building railway lines and had also, in Paris, supervised the construction of the Belleville funicular and of the Avenue de la République. With his drive and enthusiasm and his flair for finding original and economical solutions to technical problems, the 'Father of the Métro' was responsible for the completion of the initial works in an incredibly short time. Bienvenüe continued in his post until 1932 and in the following year, the City honoured him by renaming the station Maine to Bienvenüe (now Montparnasse-Bienvenüe). He died in 1936. It was Bienvenüe who said that he wanted a Métro which would be part of the family 'qu'il puisse tutoyer' and one wonders what he would have made of the RER.

Stations built by the cut-and-cover method are recognisable by the steel girders at roof level. At Porte d'Orléans on line 4, supporting pillars separate the arrival and departure tracks. A train of MP59 stock in the original livery awaits departure, showing the new logo on the cab front. David Rowe

PARIS METRO HANDBOOK

BRIAN HARDY

Capital Transport

First published 1988
Reprinted 1990
Second edition 1993

ISBN 185414 154 6

Published by Capital Transport Publishing
38 Long Elmes, Harrow Weald, Middlesex

Printed by Winchmore Press, Ilford, Essex

Below This view of two unrefurbished trains of MP59 stock is in the extensive network of tunnels at Porte de Clignancourt, the northern terminus and stabling area of line 4. Two liveries are shown, the original one for this stock and the later royal blue and white. Julian Pepinster

Facing Page Lower The trains of MF77 stock on line 8 in the new livery are being painted, whereas those on line 7 comprise an adhesive material applied over the original finish. A train departs Créteil-Préfecture for the long journey through central Paris to Balard, on 15 January 1993. Brian Hardy

CONTENTS

AUTHOR'S NOTE

The success of the first edition of Paris Métro Handbook, published in the autumn of 1988 was followed in 1990 by a reprint, almost identical to original work. Some four years later, however, much has changed and there are ambitious plans to take the Métro and Paris transport generally forward well into the 21st century – now is the time for a new edition. This new edition also includes the RATP's Bobigny to Saint-Denis tramway (whose vehicles are maintained by the Métro) and the Montmartre funicular (which is managed as part of Métro line 2).

Plans that were still on paper four years ago are now turning into reality, with a brand new Métro line (Météor) now under construction, as well as a northerly extension on line 13 from Saint-Denis-Basilique to Saint-Denis-Université. Even grander schemes exist for the suburban railways (SNCF) and the Regional Express network (RER), but (in the case of the latter) more of that in another future publication.

On the rolling stock side, delivery of new trains based on the 'BOA' prototype for line 7bis has commenced. A large order for new rubber-tyred trains has also been placed for line 1 and the new Météor line now being built.

The inspiration for Paris Métro Handbook came from the LRTL (now LRTA) book 'On Rails Under Paris' by the late B.J. Prigmore, published in 1970 and 1974, which generated a new interest for your writer, to the extent that what was originally intended to be a once-only visit to Paris, has resulted in countless visits since!

In preparing this second edition I wish to express my thanks to Brian Patton, who has continued to do a magnificent job in translating numerous documents from French into English, Bert Steinkamp, who continues to share his intimate and detailed knowledge of the Paris Métro of some 35 years, and John Thomason, for ensuring that all the 'accents' are in the right places. In Paris, help from Julian Pepinster and the late Pascal Lesure is gratefully acknowledged. But without the help and encouragement from the Paris Métro Authority (RATP), this work would not be so extensive and grateful thanks are expressed to Messrs Decreusefond, Millot and Pigault, Mme Honig from the Médiatheque, and to the many RATP staff who so willingly and patiently answered what must have seemed numerous and almost never-ending questions. A special word of thanks must go to M. Sampeur of the RATP, who not only guided me around many parts of the Métro network, but also made many facilities and documents available to me. This book would not have been possible without the help of Jeanne, who even agreed to spend Christmas Day taking photographs! If, unintentionally, I have failed to acknowledge the contributions of anyone else, then I apologise in advance.

BRIAN HARDY

Ickenham, Middlesex.
February 1993.

Front Cover **Since the first edition of this handbook was published all of the MP59 stock trains have been repainted and refurbished. In this May 1992 photograph of a train departing from Bastille, the new RATP logo can be seen.** Brian Hardy

Work on the construction of line 1 began in November 1898 and went ahead so rapidly that, after some weeks of trial running, it was opened for traffic without ceremony at 13.00 on 19 July 1900. After some hesitation, both Parisians and visitors took to the new system with such enthusiasm that the number of passengers carried rose from 1.8 million in August to almost 4 million in December 1900. Thus encouraged, the City pressed on with the building of new lines and the original network was completed more than a year ahead of schedule, in January 1910. Long before that date, however, plans for further extensions had been made. Bienvenüe was consistently aware of the need to plan the system as a whole – in his words 'Le Métro ne se refrait pas' (the Métro wouldn't happen again) and in 1901 submitted plans for two new lines, the predecessors of lines 9 and 10, plus various extensions. Two additional lines mentioned as possibilities in the original agreement were authorised in April 1902 (line 7) and April 1903 (line 8). The result of all this advance planning was that some important and difficult works, such as the crossing of lines 3, 7 and 8 at Opéra (all underground), could be carried out as one combined operation, even though certain parts would not be needed for some years.

But the progress of the CMP was not made in the security of a total monopoly. Berlier (q.v. above) had not given up his interest in tube lines and in 1901 he and one Janicot obtained from the City a concession for such a line from Montmartre to Montparnasse, which they immediately made over to the Chemin de Fer Electrique Souterrain Nord-Sud de Paris, normally referred to as the Nord-Sud. The main difference between this and the CMP's concession was that the lines were to be built at the Company's expense. It was intended that, being in tube, they would not have to follow the street pattern, but the waterlogged subsoil of Paris was a different proposition to the London clay and after a few trial borings it was decided that the Nord-Sud would have to be built by conventional Parisian methods. Construction of the main line (line A) was authorised in 1905 along with an extension to Porte de Versailles and a branch (line B) from Gare Saint-Lazare to Porte de Saint-Ouen. A third line (C) from Montparnasse to Porte de Vanves was authorised in 1912 but not built during the lifetime of the Nord-Sud company.

The stations of the Nord-Sud were more spacious than those of the CMP and were more elaborately decorated. Today, the restored circular ticket hall at Saint-Lazare shows the Company's style to advantage as does Liège (line 13). But the main difference between the two companies lay in the method of current collection. To avoid the problem of voltage drop without the building of numerous substations, the Nord-Sud was electrified on a three-wire 1,200V system. The leading motor picked up current at +600V from an overhead wire via a small pantograph and the rear motor coach took current at −600V from a third rail. In emergency both could operate from either pickup at 600V only.

Meanwhile Bienvenüe's additional network 'réseau complémentaire' had been author-ised by the City in 1910 and work on it began as soon as that on the original lines was complete. The First World War led to the suspension of construction after 1916. Apart from this, the main effect of the War on the CMP was the development of a system of electropneumatic closing of the doors, which allowed the reduction of the crew on a five coach train from six to four.

The immediate post-war period brought many difficulties in the form of rising costs and demands by crews for shorter hours. The first strike on the Métro and the first increase in fares came in 1919, despite which the CMP was unable to pay to the City the monies due in that year. After prolonged discussions, therefore, new agreements were drawn up between the City and the two companies under which the former undertook financial responsibility for the two systems, the companies receiving in return a fixed price of 1.7 centimes per ticket sold. As the Département of the Seine had just acquired the various tramway companies, and thereby also the Compagnie Générale des Omnibus, local government was now in control of most of the city's transport. Unfortunately while the Métro was controlled by the City, the newly-formed Sociéte des Transports en Commun de la Région Parisienne was the responsibility of the Département of the Seine and was much better placed to compete with the Métro than the individual tramway companies had been. With financial stability restored, work on the new lines was resumed and the secondary network was redefined in a plan of 1922, much of it being brought into service between 1925 and 1930.

The inter-war years were marked by a spectacular growth of the inner suburban area and by 1931 its population was almost equal to that of the city itself. For the first time commuter traffic to and from the suburbs assumed major importance and this led to congestion both at the outer termini of the Métro and at the main-line stations. The original concept of a purely urban system was clearly no longer appropriate and in October 1929 three new agreements were signed by the City, the Département and the two companies. Under these the CMP regained much of its former financial autonomy, the Département agreed to construct fifteen extensions into the suburbs, to be worked as part of the Métro and a separate fare system for the suburban area was to be created. The price exacted by the authorities for this agreement was the fusion of the Nord-Sud with the CMP and this duly took place on 1 January 1930. In the following year the two Nord-Sud lines were converted to the CMP system of current collection.

Work on the suburban extensions began immediately and the majority were brought into operation between 1934 and 1937, while two new urban lines were also built. But in spite of the growth of the network, the 1930s were a period of declining traffic and there was clearly over-capacity in local transport in Paris. As local authorities were unwilling to take responsibility for increasing fares or reducing services, the national government stepped in and in November 1938 appointed a committee to co-ordinate transport in the Paris area. The outbreak of war and the subsequent political upheaval delayed implementation of plans but once matters had settled down after the start of German occupation, the Vichy government in June 1941 passed a Law amalgamating the CMP and the STCRP with effect from 1 January 1942. In practice the Métro took over the bus system (the last tram had run in 1938) or at least those parts of it which were still extant. As the Second World War progressed, bus services were reduced for want of fuel and for most of 1944 and 1945 there were no buses running within the city and only a very few in the suburbs. As a result the Métro had to cope with tremendous overcrowding. To help ease the situation, redundant staff were transferred from the road section and overhaul times for rolling stock were reduced. Remarkably the system coped without any major breakdown. There was little physical damage to the Métro during the War, although a few cars were destroyed by none-too-accurate Allied bombing of military targets in 1944. In the weeks immediately before the liberation of Paris, the system came to a complete standstill and reopening was a gradual process during the autumn of 1944.

The provisional arrangement made in 1941 was not altogether satisfactory and had in any case been pushed through without any reference to local authorities and with no provision for democratic control. It was also thought that the officers of the CMP had been rather too co-operative with the Vichy authorities and with the occupying forces, both in allowing the latter to use workshop facilities and in applying the anti-Communist and anti-semitic policies of the former. Members of the resistance had been found mainly among the workers, rather than in the higher echelons of the CMP. As a result, in January 1945, the Minister of Transport suspended from their functions the two principal officers of the CMP and placed the latter under a provisional administration which was in fact to last for four years. A total of 59 other employees were compulsorily retired because of their record of collaboration. In every respect the Métro suffered – from its own success in coping with the war traffic, from the association of its officers with the Vichy government and from the sheer necessity of first rebuilding the shattered system of road transport. All these factors help to explain its relative neglect by the authorities in the post-war years.

The various governments which were in power after the end of the War made strenuous attempts to find a solution to the question of the city's transport, but it was not until 1947 that agreement was reached on a future structure, finally created by a Law of 21 March 1948. This provided for two new bodies; the 'Office Régionale des Transports Parisiens' was intended to co-ordinate services, including those of the SNCF, to draw up plans for the future and to fix fares, the 'Régie Autonome des Transports Parisiens' was responsible for the operation of the combined systems of the Métro and road transport. Apart from the replacement of the ORTP by the 'Syndicat des Transports Parisiens' in 1959, the administrative structure created in 1948 has lasted to the present day, though in recent years the regional planning commission has played an increasing role in transport affairs. The RATP was from the start required both to provide a public service and to balance its budget, but this was not possible after 1953 and the result was an almost total cessation of investment, which particularly affected the Métro. No increases in fares were allowed by the ORTP between August 1951 and February 1958 and the result was a deficit which annually grew to reach 16.4 milliard old francs in 1957. The very small amounts which were made available to the RATP for investment in its rail system were used to finance the extension of line 13, the experiments with trains running on pneumatic tyres and with the modernisation of the station lighting by the use of fluorescent tubes. But despite this stagnation, the number of passengers continued to grow and in 1959 reached 1,200 million.

By 1959 it was clear that affairs could not continue in this manner and the government of the Fifth Republic, by a decree of 7 January 1959, replaced the ORTP by the new Syndicat des Transports, with wide powers over investment. In 1962 a new financial arrangement was concluded with the RATP. Under a rather complicated formula, the RATP prepares a balanced budget and any deficit resulting from failure to raise fares to the level necessary to achieve this is made good by the public authorities. Unfortunately the years of stagnation left the administrators unprepared to cope with a strategy of investment and there were considerable problems, mostly affecting the building of the RER but also concerned with the very troubled introduction of 'pneu' stock to line 1, which had caused something of a commuters' revolt. In December 1963, the Minister of Transport dismissed the Director-General of the RATP and replaced him with Pierre Weil, external relations officer of the SNCF.

The arrival of Weil marked the turning point in the post-war fortunes of the Métro. He was both the first Director-General who had not come from either the CMP or the STCRP and he was also the first of sufficient stature to cope with the problems of the RATP. In 1964 he set up a division for new works 'Direction des Travaux Neufs' and began a vigorous campaign to recruit engineers and technicians of calibre to the RATP. While the main effort had to be directed towards the construction of the RER, it was also possible once again to consider extensions to the Métro and the investment programme for 1965–67 included the extension of lines 3, 8 and 13. Weil also decided to abandon the programme of conversion to rubber-tyred trains, a programme which would not have been completed even now, and to introduce a modern version of the Classic stock. A first order for 200 cars of this stock, the MF 67, was placed in 1966. But it was recognised that the rubber-tyred trains still posed many advantages for a new system and the RATP's subsidiary SOFRETU, which had been set up in 1961, was responsible for the construction and equipment of the metros in Montréal (1966), Mexico City (1969) and Santiago de Chile (1971).

Alongside the extensions and the new rolling stock, the period also saw the development of many techniques which revolutionised the operation of the Métro. Centralisation of control, automatic operation of trains and automation of the issue and control of tickets all date from these years. When Pierre Weil resigned from his post in December 1971, having expressed doubts about the wisdom of interconnecting the RER with lines of the SNCF, he left the Métro in a much better position than he had found it eight years earlier. His successor Pierre Giraudet continued his policies and pursued a vigorous programme of extensions of the Métro into the suburbs, on the basis of a rolling programme for the next fifteen years.

The years after 1980 were marked by a certain degree of instability as successive governments sought to increase control over the capital's transport. On the other hand, a Law of 4 August 1982, which made employers responsible for meeting first 40%, then 50% of the cost of commuting led to a further growth in traffic and the period also saw an increasing pursuit of research into topics such as the 'BOA' train, which are set to bear fruit in the 1990s. It has indeed been fortunate that the activities of the RATP, and perhaps especially those of the Métro, have generally been the subject of a great degree of social consensus and that all political parties have been supportive of public transport. The plans for the future outlined in a later chapter, will show how this support will be translated into action in the 1990s.

Above **The new logo of the Paris Transport Authority, which can now be found on its trains and buses. Using artistic licence, it represents a 'green' City of Paris through which a blue River Seine meanders in the shape of a human face looking up towards the future.** RATP

Right **Map of the Paris Métro system showing the dense network of lines in the city centre.** RATP

CHAPTER TWO
THE DEVELOPMENT OF THE NETWORK

Line 1

The premier line of the Métro – its original line – is line 1, which was opened on 19 July 1900 from Porte de Vincennes to Porte Maillot, running roughly on an east to west axis. At both terminal stations, separate island platforms for arrival and departure were provided, being connected by a sharply-curved single-track loop, which avoided the need for trains to reverse. Apart from Bastille station, where it crosses over the Saint-Martin canal, the line operates in tunnel. The western end of Bastille station has the severest passenger curve on the whole of the Métro at 40m radius. Operation remained unchanged until an extension was opened beyond the city boundary from Porte de Vincennes to Château de Vincennes on 24 March 1934. The old terminal station at Porte de Vincennes was retained for the extension, but in later years the layout was altered to have one track in each direction. The original arrangement can be observed to this day, with the extra wide platforms. A westward extension was made to Pont de Neuilly on 29 April 1937, but prior to that, new platforms had been constructed at Porte Maillot and brought into use on 15 November 1936, in anticipation of the extension.

The old Classic stock was replaced by pneumatic-tyred trains, making their debut on 30 May 1963. The changeover in stock was completed by December 1964. Although line 11 had been converted to 'pneu' operation from 1957, line 1 was the first major Métro line to be so converted. This was far from simple, particularly as there was a tendency to drive the new stock like a Sprague train. Also, it was very hard for a Sprague train to keep up with the new stock.

A new western extension to line 1 was opened on 1 April 1992, from Pont de Neuilly to La Défense, the latter (already being served by RER line A) being named 'Grande Arche de La Défense' from its opening. On leaving Pont de Neuilly, the line rises sharply to the surface and runs in the middle of Route Nationale 14, crossing the River Seine. On the west side of the Pont de Neuilly, the line goes underground, where immediately the intermediate station of Esplanade de La Défense is located. The line then continues underground in cut-and-cover tunnels but on an uphill gradient to Grande Arche de La Défense, where terminating trains continue on to reverse, as the arrival and departure platforms are in completely separate locations, above the tracks of the RER on each side of the mezzanines. The present length of line 1 is 16.5km and in 1991 it continued to be the Métro's third busiest line, carrying over 108.7 million passengers.

Line 2

Line 2 originally began as a shuttle from Étoile (now Charles de Gaulle-Étoile) to Porte Dauphine on 13 December 1900. The latter terminus is similar to the original line 1 terminus at Porte Maillot, the arrival and departure platforms being linked by a sharply-curved loop of 30m radius. The first part of the main portion of the line was opened from Étoile to Anvers on 7 October 1902, followed by the section onwards to Bagnolet (renamed Alexandre Dumas in 1970) on 31 January 1903. This latter section comprises 2.22km on viaduct, with four elevated stations (Barbès-Rochechouart, La Chapelle, Stalingrad and Jaurès), and crosses the main line exits from the Gare du Nord and Gare de l'Est. (At Gare du Nord, recent lengthening work on the SNCF main line platforms in connection with the future Channel Tunnel trains has now seen them finish actually under the Métro bridge between La Chapelle and Barbès-Rochechouart). The last section onwards to Nation was completed on 2 April 1903 and the pattern of service has remained unchanged since then, though it should be mentioned that the line was known as 2 Nord (North) until 14 October 1907, from when it became line 2. The length of line is 12.316km, and operates wholly within the city boundary.

This night-time view shows work proceeding on the construction of the line 1 extension at Esplanade de La Défense in November 1991, with the trackwork already in place. It shows that the line is constructed in the middle of Autoroute A14. Looking eastwards, the illuminated Eiffel Tower can just be seen in the centre and the Arc de Triomphe at far left. Brian Hardy

Later, on the opposite side of the line at Esplanade de La Défense on 3 May 1992, much work remains to be done as illustrated in the foreground, but the extension is operational with a train of refurbished MP59 stock arriving. Again, the Arc de Triomphe can be seen in the background. Jeanne Gill

Line 2 runs in the open-air between Jaurès and Barbès-Rochechouart on overhead viaduct. In this view, west of Jaurès, the line curves sharply towards the next station, Stalingrad. A train of MF67E stock negotiates this curve under the watchful eye of the Sacre Coeur in the background. Brian Hardy

Now that some of the SNCF's main line platforms at Gare du Nord have been lengthened to accommodate the future Channel Tunnel trains, they now extend up to the bridge where line 2 passes over, between La Chapelle and Barbès-Rochechouart, as seen on 10 May 1992. Brian Hardy

When line 3 was extended eastwards to Galliéni, new platforms were built at Gambetta, slightly west of the old station. As this was very close to adjacent Martin Nadaud station, its platforms were used for one of the many entrances to the station complex and effectively closed. This view of the new station shows the remains of the old station in the background. Brian Hardy

Line 3

Rather oddly, line 3 was not the next line to be opened (line 5 in fact got in before 3 and 4) and was inaugurated in stages, as follows:

Villiers to Père-Lachaise	19 October 1904
Père-Lachaise to Gambetta	25 January 1905
Villiers to Péreire	23 May 1910
Péreire to Porte de Champerret	15 February 1911

This line was the first to open after the Couronnes disaster (q.v. Rolling Stock) and incorporated improved safety features devised in the light of the experience gained from that. There was a system of emergency lighting for the tunnels, the wires for which were buried in the ballast, and the stations had improved emergency facilities. Villiers station was a terminus for just over five years and trains reversed in sidings away from the subsequent alignment to Champerret. These sidings beyond the station continue to be used for instructional purposes for train drivers. Line 3 was further extended at the eastern side of the city from Gambetta to Porte des Lilas on 27 November 1921. It was extended in the western suburbs, to Pont de Levallois on 24 September 1937.

A major upheaval in the line's history came in 1971 when the section from Gambetta to Porte des Lilas became a self-contained branch line (3bis) on 27 March in connection with the opening of an extension from Gambetta to a new transport interchange complex at Galliéni on 2 April 1971. This new extension required the provision of 'through' platforms at Gambetta. Two new platforms were thus built just west of the original station and were even closer to the adjacent station of Martin Nadaud. The distance between the old Gambetta station and Martin Nadaud had been, at 0.23km, the shortest distance between any pair of Métro stations. The new arrangement saw the access via Martin Nadaud

One of several short extensions of the mid-1930s took line 3 from Porte de Champerret to Pont de Levallois, constructed in a style used over many years previously — tiled and enamel station names, tiled advert surrounds and white bevelled tiling survive here to this day. Brian Hardy

retained (its old platforms still serve as a link to the new Gambetta platforms), while the old island platform at Gambetta in the Paris direction became the terminus for line 3bis – the other platforms were demolished, but the careful observer will notice (just) the remains of the old tiled walls of the station, on leaving Gambetta heading towards Galliéni. Line connections continue to exist at Gambetta between the branch and the main line and trains from line 3 are stabled at night at Porte des Lilas, running empty from Gambetta.

Line 3 was the first to receive modern steel-wheel trains from late-1967, but 3bis continued to operate the old Classic stock until 2 July 1981. The main line is now 11.684km long and the branch 1.289km – all of it underground.

Line 4

The unexpected difficulties found in the construction of a tunnel under the River Seine meant that line 4 was, unusually, originally opened as two disconnected pieces. The northern section between Porte de Clignancourt and Châtelet was the first to open on 21 April 1908, while the southern section between Porte d'Orléans and Raspail followed on 30 October 1909. The two sections were finally connected on 9 January 1910 and the line has not been extended since then, a 1928 proposal for an extension from the southern terminus to Carrefour de la Vache Noire not having been pursued. However, a 330m long deviation of the line was made from 3 October 1977 in connection with a new station at Les Halles, 30m to the east, to make interchange with the enormous RER complex easier.

Conversion to pneumatic-tyred trains took place between October 1966 and July 1967. This line, 10.598km long and all underground, is presently the busiest on the Métro, carrying over 127 million passengers in 1991.

What are now the terminal platforms for line 5 at Place d'Italie used to be 'through' platforms when the line operated from (then) Étoile to Gare du Nord until 1942. From then, line 6 assumed the Étoile to Place d'Italie (and on to Nation) section, while line 5 was extended at its northern end to Église de Pantin. Brian Hardy

Lines 5 and 6

The second Métro line to be opened was what is now line 6, from Étoile to Trocadéro on 2 October 1900. This line was at first known as line 2 Sud (South) and was extended from Trocadéro to Passy on 6 November 1903 and on to Place d'Italie on 24 April 1906. There it was soon joined by line 5, whose first section from Place d'Italie to Gare d'Orléans (now Gare d'Austerlitz) was opened on 2 June of the same year. Line 5 had been originally intended to run from the Gare de l'Est to the Pont d'Austerlitz via the Gare de Lyon, but it soon became obvious that this would involve an impossibly steep gradient from the latter station up to the viaduct over the River Seine, and the line as built was diverted to the west to run via Quai de la Rapée (at that date known as Place Mazas and renamed Pont d'Austerlitz from 1907 to 1916), a connection being provided to the Gare de Lyon. It was then decided that line 5 should incorporate the section on to Place d'Italie originally intended to have been part of line 2 Sud, and this was in fact the first portion to be opened. Line 5 was extended to Place Mazas on 14 July 1906, from which date a connecting shuttle service was provided to Gare de Lyon. From 1 August 1906 this was replaced by a through service with trains having to reverse at Place Mazas, but when a northbound extension to Lancry (now Jacques Bonsergent) was opened on 17 December 1906, the service to Gare de Lyon was abandoned, leaving this station rather isolated on line 1 until the RER was built some seventy years later. The abandoned section served, between 1937 and 1967, as the 'finance line', where a double-ended motor car collected cash from stations to be taken to Gare de Lyon. It still serves to transfer rolling stock between lines 1 and 5, and also is used for instructional purposes for train drivers.

The use of Place d'Italie as a terminus for lines 2 Sud and 5 was inconvenient for both operating staff and passengers and on 14 October 1907 the lines were amalgamated under the latter number. From the same date, line 2 Nord became line 2. A northward extension to the Gare du Nord followed on 15 November 1907, after which the service remained unchanged for many years, although from 17 May to 6 December 1931, during the period of the Colonial Exhibition, it was curtailed to run from Place d'Italie to Gare du Nord.

Gare d'Austerlitz station on line 5 is in fact located in the roof of part of the SNCF station, where a train of MF67 stock is seen entering. Brian Hardy

The CMP was not particularly enthusiastic about line 6 in the early days, as it did not promise to generate much traffic and, though the infrastructure was completed by the City from Place d'Italie through to Nation in 1906, the Company took refuge in a clause in the original agreement which said that lines should be opened in the order they were listed therein and consequently they did not begin to operate line 6 until after the first section of line 4 had been placed in service. The actual opening date was 1 March 1909. The line was briefly extended to Étoile in 1931 in place of line 5 (q.v. above).

An extension of line 5 from Gare du Nord to Église de Pantin was under construction in 1939 but the opening was delayed by the outbreak of the Second World War and it was not until 6 October 1942 that new platforms were opened at Gare du Nord on the alignment of the extension. The extension itself was brought into operation on 12 October 1942. As line 5 would then have become too long for reasonable operation, it was, from the same date, curtailed to terminate at Place d'Italie. The section between Place d'Italie and Étoile was transferred to line 6, also on 12 October 1942, and this line then described a southern arc of the City. The former line 5 terminus at Gare du Nord is used for train driver instruction.

Much of line 6 is in the open air – in stark contrast to other early Métro lines. Over 6km of the 13.624km route length is on viaduct. Line 5 is mostly in the open from north of Campo-Formio to just beyond Quai de la Rapée, and this section is most interesting to the enthusiast. Climbing onto an elevated structure, the station of Gare d'Austerlitz is located in the roof of the SNCF station. The line then crosses the River Seine on the Austerlitz bridge before curving and descending sharply into tunnel, in which the connection to and from Gare de Lyon on line 1 is situated, and then rising again to the surface at Quai de la Rapée. Not surprisingly, this section has earned the title of 'the toboggan'. On leaving Quai de la Rapée station the line immediately crosses the Saint Martin canal and then continues underground.

Line 6 was converted for pneumatic-tyred trains between October 1972 and May 1974. In comparison to other 'pneu' conversions, line 6 was undertaken mainly for environmental reasons, to reduce noise on the open sections of the line. The rolling stock was changed over from July 1974. It was originally intended that the conversion of line 2 would similarly follow and that the two lines would be linked, making one large circular service, but this plan has now been abandoned.

After over forty years of unchanged operation, line 5 was extended in 1985, from Église de Pantin to Bobigny - Pablo Picasso, opening on 25 April, with one intermediate station named Bobigny Pantin - Raymond Queneau and increasing the length of line 5 from

11.2km to 14.629km. Among the problems encountered with the construction of this extension was the severe flooding on 6 June 1982 which filled, and subsequently burst through, the new workings, and onto the existing Métro system at Église de Pantin. Here, 18 trains that were stabled were severely damaged by the immense torrent of water, all of which had to receive major workshop attention. On the new extension, the route crosses the Paris-Strasbourg main line and the Ourcq canal, both underground. Part of the line, between Bobigny Pantin and Bobigny-Pablo Picasso, is in the open and stabling sidings were built on the north side of the line, which has accommodation for over two-thirds of the rolling stock for line 5. A maintenance depot has also been built, which opened in April 1988. The depot also maintains the trams which operate at street level from Bobigny to La Courneuve (opened 6 July 1992) with a further extension to Saint-Denis opened on 21 December 1992.

The distance between the two Bobigny stations, at 2.43km, is now the longest inter-station section on the Métro network.

Southwards from Gare d'Austerlitz, line 5 runs on viaduct, as seen here, before going underground to the next station, Saint-Marcel. In this view, the prototype 'BOA' train is seen in service and illustrates the three different inter-vehicle connections employed. RATP

Although the western terminus of line 6 is at Charles de Gaulle – Étoile, the layover time is taken at Kléber, because of the former being on a single line loop. Charles de Gaulle – Étoile illustrated here has separate platforms for detraining (right) and entraining (left).
Brian Hardy

The present line 6 operates for about half of its length on elevated viaducts and was thus an ideal choice to convert to quieter rubber-tyred train operation. A five-car train arrives at Quai de la Gare on 10 July 1992. Picture Account

In 1967 the section of line 7 between Louis Blanc and Pré-Saint-Gervais became an independent line — line 7bis. Today the line is operated by four-car trains of MF67E stock. At Louis Blanc terminus, as illustrated here, cross platform interchange is made between trains on lines 7 (left) and 7bis (right). Brian Hardy

Line 7

The history of line 7 is perhaps the most complex of any Métro line. It was originally intended that it should run from Opéra to a terminus in the north-east of the City, but the municipal authorities were unable to decide on the exact location of this terminus and in the end it was arranged that it should in fact take the form of a large loop, which would incorporate all of the proposed stations. It was later decided to add a branch to Porte de la Villette. The presence of old underground quarry workings under the Buttes-Chaumont caused problems in the construction of the line in that area and the first section to be opened was in fact from Opéra to Porte de la Villette on 5 November 1910. The line from Louis Blanc to Pré-Saint-Gervais was added on 18 January 1911. This was the first 'branch' of the Métro in the true sense and trains ran in an anti-clockwise direction round the loop. The outbreak of the First World War in 1914 delayed the opening of an extension from Opéra to Palais-Royal until 1 July 1916, although the work on the stations had not quite been finished even then. Extensions onwards to Pont Marie followed on 16 April 1926, to Sully Morland on 3 June 1930 and to Place Monge on 26 April 1931. The line thence south to Porte de Choisy had already been opened for traffic on 7 March 1930 and had been worked temporarily on an extension of line 10. It now assumed its intended role as part of line 7 and was extended to Porte d'Ivry, also on 26 April 1931. One of the few extensions to the Métro in the immediate post-war period took line 7 further south from Porte d'Ivry to Mairie d'Ivry on 1 May 1946.

At the northern end of line 7, the branch line to Pré-Saint-Gervais became a self-contained service as line 7bis from 3 December 1967, to allow a more frequent service to operate to Porte de la Villette. Whilst the main line received new rolling stock from June 1971, the branch 7bis continued to operate Classic stock until July 1980. Five-car trains of MF67F stock then took over, being replaced by four-car trains of type MF67E in 1984, which continues to operate the service today.

Although one of the Métro's longer lines for many years, a number of extensions have been made to line 7. In the north, a two-station extension from Porte de la Villette to Fort d'Aubervilliers was made on 4 October 1979. At the southern end the first stage of a new branch reached Le Kremlin-Bicêtre on 10 December 1982 and although it was the intention to serve each branch with alternate trains, it was soon found necessary to operate a pattern in the evening peaks so that Mairie d'Ivry had two trains to Le Kremlin-Bicêtre's one, because of the uneven traffic flows. This situation was rectified when the ultimate southern terminus of Villejuif-Louis Aragon was reached on 28 February 1985. Trains were then able to serve the two southern branches alternately, and indeed, both have identical running times from end to end. The final extension to line 7 was opened to the public on 6 May 1987, when the northern terminus was extended one station to La Courneuve – 8 Mai 1945. With a total route length of 22.8km, line 7 is now the longest of all Métro lines and is the second busiest line, carrying over 111 million passergers in 1991. Line 7 also operates the most trains in service (65) at peak times. Both line 7 and branch line 7bis (3.066km) are wholly underground.

At Opéra, lines 3, 7 and 8 cross, all underground. This view shows line 8 (lower right), line 7 (left), above which can be seen the girder work for line 3. RATP

Trains on line 7bis operate in an anti-clockwise direction around the Pré-Saint-Gervais loop. All three stations on this loop have two platforms, but only one at each is used by passengers. The island platform at Place des Fêtes shows that only the left-hand platform is in use, being fitted with seats and lighting, also the tactile strip at platform edge for blind and partially sighted passengers. Brian Hardy

Most of the Métro extensions since 1970 have been built by the cut-and-cover method and thus the stations are in a rectangular box shape. The northern terminus of line 7 is at La Courneuve – 8 Mai 1945 and opened on 6 May 1987. This station now has interchange with the tramway to Bobigny which opened on 6 July 1992. A further extension of the tramway to Saint-Denis opened on 21 December 1992. Brian Hardy

Lines 8, 9 and 10

The history of these three lines is also rather complex, and as they were planned and, to a certain extent, built together, they will be dealt with as a group.

Line 8 was mentioned in the first plans, but only as a line which should be constructed at a later date. It was finally agreed in 1903 that it should be built from the Opéra to Auteuil, with a branch to Porte de Sèvres (now Place Balard). However, before any work was done, the line became merged in a much grander scheme. In 1907 the municipal authorities adopted a plan for an additional network, to follow the construction of the main system. This plan included the first part of line 9 and also an inner circle, to run from Invalides to Invalides via the Boulevard Saint Germain, Bastille, République and Opéra. Between République and Invalides this line would share the tracks of line 8 to which line 9 might also be added. It was also planned that line 8 would include a connection to line 9 at the southern end to allow trains on both lines to serve both termini. It was all a very far cry from the lines that were already in operation, with their simple end-to-end services. Fortunately, the City and the CMP later had second thoughts – perhaps someone came to London and had a close look at the complex workings of the Inner Circle! – and the grand design was never put into operation. However, it did influence both the course of the lines under discussion and the layout of the tracks in various places, such as in the vicinity of Invalides station, and it is therefore important to bear in mind what the original plans were.

Left **The visitor to the Paris Métro should include a trip on line 10 around the Auteuil loop, where trains in the outward direction pass through Mirabeau station with its single platform for inbound trains. A train of MA52 articulated stock is seen climbing the ramp through the station.** Jeanne Gill

Right **In 1937 line 10 took over the section of line 8 between La Motte-Picquet and Porte d'Auteuil for which two additional platforms (lines 8 and 10 in the westbound direction) were required. A train of MA52 stock on line 10 pauses at the latter in November 1991.** Jeanne Gill

Line 8 was inaugurated on 13 July 1913 when the section from Opéra to Beaugrenelle (named Charles Michels since 1945) was opened to traffic. It was extended to Porte d'Auteuil in the form of an anti-clockwise loop on 30 September of the same year. The eastern end was extended from Opéra to Richelieu-Drouot on 30 June 1928 and further to Porte de Charenton on 5 May 1931 in time to serve the Colonial Exhibition of that year, held in what is now called the Musée des Arts Africains et Océaniens at Porte Dorée. In 1937 there was a major re-arrangement of the south-western end of the line, which was diverted at La Motte-Picquet and extended to Balard, its previous operation to Auteuil being taken over by line 10. A south-eastern extension was opened on 5 October 1942 from Porte de Charenton to Charenton-Ecoles.

After a long period of stagnation on the Métro generally, line 8 was the first of several lines to be extended in the 1970s. Four separate stages took the line from Charenton-Écoles to Créteil-Préfecture, as follows:

Charenton-Écoles to Maisons-Alfort-Stade	19 September 1972
Maisons-Alfort-Stade to Maisons-Alfort-les Juilliottes	27 April 1972
Maisons-Alfort-les Juilliottes to Créteil-l'Echat	26 September 1973
Créteil-l'Echat to Créteil-Préfecture	10 September 1974

This extension differed from all previous extensions in that the distance between stations was on average much greater (1km as against 0.5km) and also because for the first time a supplementary fare was levied for travel on it as proposed in the 1929 plans. Supplementary fares have, however, since 1 November 1982, been discontinued. The open-air section to Créteil is, unusually, built in the central reservation of a motorway and the space for three tracks has been provided throughout. On only some of the route from Maisons-Alfort-les Juilliottes to Créteil-Préfecture has a third track actually been provided. The intention is to operate semi-fast working if desired at a later date, but for the moment, the third (western) track is used for stabling trains. Line 8 is 22.05km long.

Line 9 was originally seen as a branch of what was then line 2 Sud from Trocadéro to Porte de Saint-Cloud. In 1907, however, it was decided that it should be extended inwards to Opéra as an independent line. Then for a brief period it was envisaged that it would be worked as a branch of the proposed inner circle. Finally, it was evident that this would overload the circle and the line was constructed on its own. The exact location of the terminal sidings at Porte de Saint-Cloud caused problems and construction was delayed not only by the outbreak of war, but also by a collapse of the workings at Place de l'Alma on 8 November 1915 and by the post-war financial troubles of the CMP. The first section, from Exelmans to Trocadéro, was therefore not opened to the public until 8 November

The complex layout between lines 8 and 9 at République necessitated separate platforms instead of the normal arrangement. On line 9, a train of MF67 stock in original livery is seen and shows that the platforms here are much longer at 105 metres. Note the TV monitors suspended from the ceiling for the driver.
Jeanne Gill

1922. It was extended inwards to Saint-Augustin on 27 May 1923, to Chaussée d'Antin on 3 June 1923 and outwards to Porte de Saint-Cloud from Exelmans on 29 September of the same year. When the last part of the line was opened, it was planned that for special events at what is now the Parc des Princes stadium, alternate trains would be diverted south of Jasmin on to what was then line 8 (now line 10) via the Auteuil loop at a special station at Porte Molitor. This island platform station was completed at track level but no connection had been made to street level when the project was abandoned, as it had been decided to keep lines 8 and 9 quite separate. From Porte Molitor trains would have returned to line 9 via a large loop near Porte de Saint-Cloud. The section of line concerned is now used for stabling trains from line 9, being part of a maze of tunnels in the area. Another proposal for line 9 which was not carried out was for a branch line from Saint-Augustin to Place des Ternes on line 2. At the former, the 'wide' platform in the eastbound direction is a relic of these plans, which has been used, on occasions, for exhibition purposes.

In the inner area, lines 8 and 9 were extended together, but on separate tracks, to Richelieu-Drouot on 30 June 1928, this section being originally planned as part of the inner circle. From there, tunnels for both lines, with separate tracks, were constructed onwards to République, not without considerable opposition from property owners along the line of the Grands Boulevards, and line 9 was extended to Porte de Montreuil on 10 December 1933. The south-western terminus became Pont de Sèvres on 3 February 1934 (in fact the very first Métro extension beyond the City boundary) and the final extension in the east to Mairie de Montreuil followed on 14 October 1937.

The total length of line 9, at 19.565km, has been unchanged since 1937 and all of it operates underground. Line 9 was the last of all to operate the old Classic stock, the last trains running on 16 April 1983.

When construction work began on line 10 in 1913, it was still envisaged that this line would ultimately form part of the proposed inner circle and it was not until 1922, by which time a large junction layout had been constructed at Invalides, that it was decided that it should instead be confined to the Left Bank of the Seine. It was opened from Invalides to Croix Rouge (the latter station, situated between Sèvres-Babylone and Mabillon, is now closed) on 30 December 1923 and traffic levels were at first derisory, since their two termini were not very far apart and the intermediate stations served no very recognisable flow of passengers. It was extended one station to Mabillon on 10 March 1925 and on to Odéon on 14 February 1926. To work line 10 more economically, a series of motor coaches with driving cabs at both ends, capable of running as single units, was placed into service from December 1926.

Line 10 was extended briefly to Place d'Italie on 15 February 1930 and to Porte de Choisy on 7 March 1931. These extensions brought it an increased but unbalanced traffic. When line 7 reached the Left Bank, it assumed operation of the new section to Porte de Choisy and line 10 was instead diverted to terminate at Jussieu, reached on 26 April 1931.

With another fairly drastic re-arrangement, carried out between 26 and 29 July 1937, line 10 was extended at Duroc over a newly-built section of track to La Motte-Picquet, then by the tracks of the former line 8 to Porte d'Auteuil. The section northwards to Invalides was handed over to a new line 14. At the eastern end, line 10 was extended from Jussieu to Gare d'Austerlitz on 12 July 1939, a distance of 1.03km, making this the longest distance between two stations until the extensions of the 1970s. Nevertheless, this is still the longest distance on the Métro within the City boundary.

Line 10 was then to remain unaltered until the opening of a western extension to Boulogne - Jean Jaurès on 3 October 1980, and to Boulogne - Pont de Saint-Cloud on 2 October 1981. Initially, with the exception of the evening service, alternate trains continued to terminate at Porte d'Auteuil, giving the northern section of the one-way loop a through service into Paris. In the evenings, all trains work through to Boulogne - Pont de Saint-Cloud and passengers for Paris have first to travel to Boulogne - Jean-Jaurès and change trains there; cross platform interchange is timetabled. Since 8 April 1991 however, the Monday to Friday service to Boulogne has been improved, with two in three trains working through and every third continuing to terminate at Porte d'Auteuil in the peaks. The off peak service sees all trains work through, except during the afternoon, where it is generally two in three. All of line 10 operates underground, and is 11.708km long.

Line 11

Compared with other lines, the history of line 11 is simplicity itself. It was originally planned in 1922 and opened from Châtelet to Porte des Lilas on 28 April 1935 and one station further on to Mairie des Lilas on 17 February 1937. As it was built much later than the other lines, line 11 usually had to pass under these when it crossed them, and the sharp curves and gradients thus created made it an ideal proving ground for the operation of pneumatic-tyred trains, which went into service from 8 November 1956. The first essays of Automatic Train Operation in revenue service were also made on line 11 from September 1967 and following its success, the conversion of all its trains was completed by June 1969, the first line on the Métro to be so operated.

At a modest 6.287km in length and using four-car trains, line 11 takes just 15 minutes from one end to the other – all underground.

Line 12

Line 12 was originally line A of the Nord-Sud company and was planned as a tube from Montmartre to Montparnasse. A few preliminary soundings showed that this would be an impossible undertaking and when construction actually began in 1907, it was as a conventional underground Métro. The workings ran into the same difficulties with abandoned quarry workings as were found on line 7 of the CMP and they were further held up by a series of strikes and by the disastrous floods of January 1910. There was something of a race with the CMP who were then completing the equipping of line 7 and in the end, both lines were opened on the same day – 5 November 1910. The first section open to traffic was from Porte de Versailles to Notre-Dame-de-Lorette, and extensions northwards brought the line to Pigalle on 8 April 1911, Jules Joffrin on 31 October 1912, and Porte de la Chapelle on 23 August 1916. This last extension was opened despite a shortage of rolling stock, as the firm that was then building some additional trains was in that part of Northern France then occupied by the German army. No further extensions were made to line 12 while the Nord-Sud retained its independence. In fact, the only extension to be made in CMP days was from Porte de Versailles to Mairie d'Issy on 24 March 1934, since when the operation of line 12 has not changed. Prior to the extension to Mairie d'Issy, a new station was opened at Porte de Versailles on 1 January 1930, 100m to the south of the original station. The complete 13.888km of line 12 is in tunnel.

The two southern stations on line 13 are in the open, running alongside the SNCF main line to and from Montparnasse. Since the introduction of TGV trains, a wall to act as a baffle has been built. A train of MF77 stock departs Malakoff — Rue Etienne Dolet for the short uphill climb to the terminus at Châtillon-Montrouge. Picture Account

Lines 13 and 14

The second and, as events turned out, final Nord-Sud line was line 13 (line B), opened from Saint-Lazare to Porte de Saint-Ouen on 26 February 1911, followed on 20 January 1912 by a branch from La Fourche to Porte de Clichy, trains serving each destination alternately. The line served densely populated working class districts and soon built up a good level of traffic. However, there was not much demand for first class travel and in due course the first class trailer cars were converted to composite cars, in order to increase the second class accommodation, the first such vehicles on either system.

Line 14 was originally planned as line C of the Nord-Sud company, but it was not built as such. Construction did not begin until 1934 and line 14 came into service with the opening of the section from Porte de Vanves to Avenue du Maine (renamed Bienvenüe in 1942) on 21 January 1937. Further new tunnels from the latter station to Duroc were opened on 27 July 1937, on which date the section of line 10 from Duroc to Invalides was handed over to the new line 14. The terminal working arrangements at Invalides required departing trains to traverse a large loop, before taking up normal running at the first station south – Varenne.

The main line was extended from Porte de Saint-Ouen to Carrefour Pleyel on 30 June 1952, one of only two such short extensions to the Métro in the early-post war period, until the 'rebirth' of the Métro from the 1970s. The then new articulated MA52 stock operated on line 13 from 1952, until its transfer to line 10 in 1975–76.

One of the early plans for the RER envisaged a line linking the Gare Montparnasse with Saint-Lazare, but it was soon realised that such a link could be provided at a fraction of the cost by connecting lines 13 and 14, and operating them as a combined through service. This would relieve congestion at Saint-Lazare, which was then (and still is) the busiest Métro station, and would improve capacity on line 13 from there to the two northern branches. In addition, the expanding business centres between there and Montparnasse justified this new extension, but also allowed a 25–30% easing on line 12 between these two points.

The route taken by the line 13–14 link from Saint-Lazare was via Miromesnil, at which location the new station was built under and at right angles to that on line 9, thence to Champs-Élysées-Clemenceau (providing interchange with line 1) and to Invalides, at which station trains no longer had to traverse a large loop when travelling south.

The connection between lines 13 and 14 was actually achieved in three stages, as follows:

Saint-Lazare to Miromesnil	27 June 1973
Miromesnil to Champs-Élysées-Clémenceau	18 February 1975
Champs-Élysées-Clémenceau to Invalides	9 November 1976

When the last section was opened, the complete line became one line 13.

Not only were lines 13 and 14 joined in the centre of Paris, but extensions were being made at both northern and southern ends into the suburbs. Previously, on 20 May 1976, the northern end of the main line was extended from Carrefour Pleyel to Saint-Denis-Basilique, and on the date that lines 13 and 14 merged, a southern extension was opened from Porte de Vanves to Châtillon-Montrouge, the last two stations on this new section being in the open air.

Thus, by the construction of a mere 7km of new Métro line, a regional link was created, which filled several awkward gaps in the existing network and provided connections with ten other Métro lines. In 1978 line 13 was the recipient of the new MF77 trains, the line being completely worked by this stock in late-1979.

The northern branch was extended from Porte de Clichy to Gabriel Péri (Asnières-Gennevilliers) on 9 May 1980, and a crossing of the River Seine is made in the open on viaduct between Mairie de Clichy and the terminus.

There are two separate operating patterns on line 13. In peak hours, the service ratio is two trains to Saint-Denis and one to Gabriel Péri, while at all other times, each destination is served alternately. The distances on line 13 from Châtillon-Montrouge to the north end terminal stations are 16.854km (Saint-Denis) and 14.77km (Gabriel Péri). A short extension is under construction to take the northern terminus one station on, from Saint-Denis-Basilique to Saint-Denis-Université, due to open in 1996.

The Shuttle (La Navette) and Abandoned Sections

The 767m long section of line between Porte de Lilas and Pré-Saint-Gervais was originally intended to be worked as part of line 3, but by the time of its opening on 27 November 1921, the CMP had decided to work it as a shuttle. A single train of two motor coaches was sufficient for the meagre traffic and even this was later replaced by a single double-ended motor coach. The original intention in 1907 was to extend line 3 in the outward direction from Gambetta to Pré-Saint-Gervais as line 3ter and to provide a connection for the opposite direction from line 7 at Place des Fêtes. To that end, between Place des Fêtes and Porte des Lilas, the platform of an intermediate station at Haxo was completed on the southern track only, but (like that at Porte Molitor between lines 9 and 10) there was no access to street level. The line was closed on the outbreak of war on 3 September 1939.

Experiments with pneumatic-tyred trains began on this line in 1951 and from 13 April 1952 the public were allowed to use the single motor coach when it was running, between the hours of 13.30 and 19.30. No service was provided when the coach was off for maintenance, which took place on a storage track at Porte des Lilas. Experiments with automatic train operation also took place on this line from 1951 onwards. Apart from sightseers and school children, there was very little traffic. The line was closed again when the trials came to an end on 31 May 1956. Since then and until 1988, it was used mainly for driver training on 'pneu' stock. The disused platforms are occasionally used for filming and the line between Haxo and Porte des Lilas is used to store some trains from line 3 outside the peaks which run empty to and from Gambetta. From 1988 part of this section of line has been used for experiments in driverless train operation – 'Automobilisation Intégrale du Mouvement des Trains' – (AIMT).

Apart from the shuttle line, other sections of Métro lines that have been abandoned over the years for passenger train working include the following:
– Porte Maillot old platforms (line 1).
– Quai de la Rapée to Gare de Lyon (between lines 5 and 1).
– Gambetta (line 3). The present public passageway between line 3bis and line 3 (inbound direction) was formerly a running tunnel.
– Les Halles (line 4) old station deviation.
– Gare du Nord old platforms (line 5).
– Between lines 5 and 6 at Place d'Italie.
– Maubert Mutualité and Place Monge (connection between lines 7 and 10).
– At Duroc (old connection between lines 10 and 14).
– Invalides loop (line 14).

Unfulfilled Plans

Leaving aside early proposals, the first line which did not pass beyond the planning stage was line G of the 1898 agreement. This line was to have run along the Left Bank from Place Valhubert to Quai de Conti. This was in fact the route taken by the Orléans Railway for its 1900 extension to the Gare d'Orsay and perhaps it had been intended only to block that piece of main-line expansionism. At all events, it was not heard of again after that line was built.

Both line 4 and line 7 were intended to cross the Seine much further to the west than their actual routes but the existence of large numbers of historic buildings obliged the City to construct rather tortuous deviations, though this did bring line 4 some useful additional traffic at Châtelet.

The original plans for the additional network envisaged a branch of line 9 from Saint-Augustin to Place des Ternes, as well as the inner circle (q.v. above). Line 4 was also to have had a peripheral extension from Porte d'Orléans to Porte de Gentilly; when the fortifications of Paris were being dismantled in 1920 it was proposed to build this line at ground level and to prolong it to Porte d'Italie as a separate line 12. When the ex-Nord-Sud line A took the number 12, the projected line was renumbered 15 but it was becoming apparent that it would generate little new traffic and it soon disappeared from the plans.

Under plans for suburban extensions made in 1930, there would have been an extension of line 4 southwards to the Carrefour de la Vache Noire, but this was dropped from plans after 1945. Nor did line 11 reach its intended terminus at Fort de Noisy, but stopped instead at Mairie des Lilas. The planned extension of line 7 to Église de Pantin was eventually built as an extension of line 5.

Three plans of the late 1960s are now in part to be realised by the construction of Météor. One was to extend line 7bis via Gare du Nord to Saint-Lazare and to link it with the branch of line 13. The second was to extend line 5 to Cité Universitaire while the third would have diverted this line to serve Gare de Lyon, avoiding the famous toboggan at Quai de la Rapée.

Another deviation which was proposed at that time is now unlikely to be realised. This would have taken line 2 to the Gare du Nord, to the great benefit of interchange passengers, but it would have cost too much and the interchange will become less important with the construction of the RER Éole line and the extension of line D.

CHAPTER THREE
STATIONS

The growth of the Métro has already been described in Chapter II, and at the beginning of September 1939 the system comprised 159km. The start of the Second World War saw the system reduced in operational size to just over 92km, with only 85 stations open to the public. Some lines were closed completely, while many stations and sections of line were closed.

Indeed, some stations encountered two or three periods of closure, but Saint Sulpice on line 4 was closed on no less than four separate occasions. At the end of 1945 there were still 73 Métro stations closed, of which 43 reopened in 1946 and 13 more in 1947. A further seven were eventually reopened in 1951, but this left a further ten still outstanding:

Arsenal (line 5)	Cluny (10)	Rennes (12)
Bel-Air (6)	Croix Rouge (10)	Saint-Martin (8 & 9)
Champ de Mars (8)	Liège (13)	Varenne (14)

Over a decade followed before two further stations were reopened: Varenne (on 24 December 1962) and Bel-Air (on 7 January 1963). However, it was on 29 June 1967 that the fate of the eight remaining stations was decided by the RATP. Two were to reopen (Liège on 20 May 1968 and Rennes on 16 September 1968, but both on Mondays to Saturdays only and until 20.00), but it was intended that the other six were to remain closed permanently. One subsequent exception to this was the station of Cluny, which later featured in plans to be linked to the Saint-Michel station complex on RER lines B and C. It reopened on 17 February 1988, named Cluny la Sorbonne.

Design and Presentation
The original stations of the CMP possessed a unity of style, which apart from reducing construction costs, would have delighted any design consultant, had there been such around in the early 1900s. The walls were lined with white tiles, relieved only by the station names which were white on a blue ground, in either tiled form or on plates, by the maroon bench seats and by advertisements, though in the general gloom these would not have been much noticed. Lighting was by clusters of incandescent lamps which were described as 'brilliant'. Having established these standards, the CMP then stuck to them for the first four decades of its existence. Although there was great consistency, stations that were built to the cut and cover method were instantly recognisable by the girders at roof level, whereas other stations had white tiles extended right over the station ceiling. It was not until 1937, by which time ideas of brilliance had obviously changed, that the first attempts were made to improve the lighting, mainly in those stations dealing with traffic to the international exhibition of that year. But neither this nor the post-war experiments with fluorescent lighting did anything for the general image of the Métro as conveyed to the public in its stations. It also did not help that the ticket collectors' booths and the ticket offices were painted black.

The Nord-Sud company had done rather better in its presentation of stations. The roofs were decorated with patterns of occasional green or brown tiles and the advertisement panels were similarly framed, with the company's N–S entwined logo incorporated in the design. Over the station tunnel mouths, similar tiles picked out the name of the terminal station then in use. This accounts for some stations on line 12 having 'Direction Montmartre' or 'Direction Montparnasse' instead of Porte de Versailles or Porte de la Chapelle, the line having opened in stages. Another interesting feature of the Nord-Sud was the rotunda forming the ticket hall of Saint-Lazare, which was of considerable merit. It is gratifying that the RATP has restored two of these stations to their former glory, Liège on line 13 and Pasteur on line 12.

A station very much in original condition is that at Louis Blanc jointly serving lines 7 and 7bis. The station still has its old white bevelled tiles and enamel nameplates. The track on the left is used by trains terminating on line 7bis while the track on the right is used for southbound trains on line 7 to Villejuif and Mairie d'Ivry. The platform at far right is disused. A similar arrangement for trains in the opposite direction applies, but the platforms there are at a lower level. Brian Hardy

Louis Blanc along with Pré-Saint-Gervais are the only two Métro stations to retain old enamel nameplates in white-on-blue. Brian Hardy

The stations of the Nord-Sud company (lines 12 and 13) boasted more decorative station finishes, some of which can still be seen today. This included green or brown tiles across the vault and above the tunnel headwall 'direction' names as illustrated on line 12 at Lamarck Caulaincourt. Brian Hardy

There are just two out of the six stations modernised experimentally in the 1950s that remain in such condition, both being at Franklin D. Roosevelt on line 9 (upper, modernised 1952) and line 1 (lower, modernised 1957), both of which have their own distinctive finish. Brian Hardy

In the early post-war years, it was recognised that the general appearance of stations was no longer in keeping with contemporary standards of design, but at first no money was available for general improvement, other than the installation of fluorescent lighting. After some unsuccessful experiments, this was developed to a reliable standard and was generally adopted in the 1950s.

The first complete rebuilding of stations was done on a very individualistic basis, the aim being to give each station its own atmosphere and to break totally with the unity of the past. Six stations were thus modernised between 1952 and 1958. The first to be so treated was Franklin D. Roosevelt on line 9, which in 1952 was completely refurbished using unpainted aluminium panelling and illuminated advertisements. This was followed in 1954 with stainless steel cladding for Opéra on line 3, while in 1955 Chaussée d'Antin (line 9) was modernised in a further different style, followed by Saint-Paul (line 1) in 1956. In 1957 the line 1 platforms at Franklin D. Roosevelt were refurbished in glass and aluminium, the remaining painted sections being rendered in orange-red and blue.

The sixth and final experimental modernisation was carried out at République on line 3

Some 70 stations were modernised in the 1960-65 period with panelling covering the original station tiles. The colour scheme was mainly brown and cream, with light green relief, as at Arts et Métiers on line 3. Note that some lighting is used to highlight the advert panels. Brian Hardy

A small number of stations in the mid-1980s were given a minor refurbishment, still using the 1960s panelling over original tilework. An example is seen at Argentine on line 1, which also illustrates the 'Tube' television monitors that were provided on a number of Métro platforms until December 1989. Brian Hardy

in 1958, and with its orange-coloured panels covering the old tilework, this set the standard for future station modernisation on the Métro. Between 1960 and 1965, therefore, some 70 stations were renovated in a unified style, which allowed greater advertising space than hitherto. The walls were sheeted with metal panels painted a deep creamy-yellow with a green relief. The station seats were an almost continuous bench in either light or dark green or wooden finish, but not surprisingly these seats often attracted those more interested in sleeping than travelling, and in later years, many were cut down to form individual seats, while others were replaced. The station names and platform 'Direction' signs were picked out in cream on a brown background and to the eyes of the British, these stations had a distinct touch of Great Western Railway flavouring about them! The station ceilings were either painted yellow, left with white tiling, or, in the case of cut and cover stations, left with the steel girders showing. Unfortunately this modernisation reduced the available platform area and brought about increased problems of cleaning and maintenance of the original tilework behind. For these reasons, the style was abandoned after 1965.

From 1969 modernisation of Métro stations saw a new style employed, replacing the old white tiles with new yellow and orange tiles instead of just covering them over. It was the deliberate policy of this style to keep the vault in darkness and to that end the platform edge lighting reflected downwards. The platforms on line 5 at République illustrate this style, although the plum bench seats and white-on-grey station names, also a feature of this style, have been replaced. Brian Hardy

The next style of renovation appeared in 1969, initially at Mouton-Duvernet on line 4, and the opportunity was seized to refurbish stations which most needed attention to tilework. In this scheme, the old white tiles were removed completely and replaced by new flat yellow-orange tiles up to 2.20 metres high on platform side walls. This section of the platform wall, including the advertisement panels, was illuminated, but the main lighting was arranged in shaded 'blocks' along the platform edge. The roof of the station remained in shadow and the overall effect was rather gloomy compared to the previous type. A further variation in station name signs appeared with this style, being white on grey. Most of these have now been replaced by the standard white on blue nameplates and the individually-shaped groups of bench seats have been replaced as well. A total of 21 stations were modernised to this design which acquired the style name of 'Mouton-Duvernet' after the prototype. It was realised at an early stage that the finished product was ' . . . not in accord . . . with fashionable ideas'.

In 1973, therefore, a design panel was set up to advise on future station modernisation policy. Its main recommendation was that the vaulted roof of the station should become a focal point of the design, instead of being left in obscurity, and that it should be indirectly lit by sodium lamps. It was also suggested that white should remain as the predominant colour but that the tiles should be relieved by two bands of similar or matching colour, at the level of the seats and on the lighting strip over the edge of the platform. A new type of bucket seating (also in matching colours) was devised to replace the wooden benches and the various items of platform furniture were also regrouped to give an impression of visual unity, making the stations look tidier. Three stations were thus modernised as trials in 1974 and met with an enthusiastic response from the public. The comments made, however, showed that there was still some desire for variety. The three stations chosen for the trials were Pont-Neuf (line 7), Ledru-Rollin (8) and Voltaire (9). In the general application of this scheme, therefore, six colours were chosen not only for variety, but to complement the luminosity of the sodium lighting. The colours used were red, lemon yellow, dark blue, lime green, orange and light brown. The scheme has not been slavishly copied in every instance, but it has been varied where necessary to suit the characteristics of a particular station. At the original cut and cover stations, for instance, the overhead steel girders have been repainted in colours matching the station furniture.

A most pleasing style of modernisation was introduced from 1974 with three prototypes, each with their own matching colour schemes. The result of this was that over the next 10 years some 93 stations were so treated, Madeleine on line 8 being one such example done in 1979. Note that the colour scheme here is yellow, as shown in the lighting fixtures, seats and their tiled bases. Another feature of this scheme was a complete reversal of the previous style, in that the vault was illuminated.
Brian Hardy

A new scheme for station modernisation was introduced from 1987, first being tried out at Stalingrad on line 7. In most cases, new tile work replaced the old but a new style of station furniture was introduced, doing away with extensive areas of tiled bases. One of the most recent stations modernised in this scheme was at Pont de Neuilly on line 1 to coincide with the extension to La Défense. This May 1992 view of the completed work shows the 'rainbow' effect on the vault and the simple but effective station seats and perches. Jeanne Gill

This programme was halted in 1985, following cuts in spending within the RATP, but not before 93 stations had been modernised in this successful style. Many stations have been extensively modernised with completely new flat tiles, while 50 other stations still retain the old bevelled tiles, which have been replaced only where necessary. Some of the latter type of stations still retain tiled station names and original tiled advert surrounds, and many stations at first equipped with sodium lighting have been re-equipped with 'white' light.

Between the various modernisation schemes, a number of experimental styles have been tried. At Odéon (line 10) the platform tiles were removed and the walls were painted in a very pale pink. Station names comprised illuminated signs, red on pale pink. This was done in 1967. Other experiments include Opéra (lines 7 and 8). Havre-Caumartin (line 9) and Saint-Lazare (lines 12 and 13), all five of which were really variations of the Mouton-Duvernet style, done in the same period, 1972-73, but differed in the colour of tiles used. Other stations to follow a similar style to the Mouton-Duvernet group include Gambetta (the new station on line 3), and Kléber, both of which have bevelled fawn-coloured tiles, the two new stations on line 13 (Miromesnil and Champs-Élysées-Clémenceau) and the modernised station at the former on line 9.

Most of the tunnel stations built since the 1970s on the Métro are instantly recognisable as being of cut and cover construction, with their rectangular boxed shape. A good deal of individuality has been shown in the design of these stations, with imagination used for lighting schemes and decoration.

The reduction of money available to modernise stations meant less grandiose products in the mid-1980's, the result being minor station renovations but often 'individualised' with small theme displays. The chance was then taken to exploit the 1960–65 style, often by painting the creamy-yellow panels white and repainting the ducting into varying colour schemes. To date, just three of the 1960–65 stations remain in the chocolate/cream style (Saint-Sulpice [line 4], Sèvres-Babylone and Jules Joffrin [12]), although 33 survive, having had the metal panels overpainted.

In 1987 the RATP began a pilot scheme in station modernisation at Stalingrad on line 7. This comprised total renovation but more cost-effective techniques and materials were used than hitherto. The result was very pleasing, with the station lighting reflecting colours onto the white tiled ceiling, giving a 'rainbow' effect. A new style of station seat (for three passengers, each separated by solid armrests to deter sleeping vagrants) has been adopted, along with lean-on perches. To date, 13 stations have been so renovated, although not all have the 'rainbow' lighting, and work is proceeding on a further line.

In addition to the many variations to station styles on the Métro, some of the specific themes at selected stations, mostly incorporated within a particular modernisation scheme, deserve a special mention. The first and perhaps most famous station is Louvre-Rivoli on line 1, so completed in 1968 (when named Louvre) with replica exhibits from the nearby Louvre Museum, indirectly lit against a restful background of cream coloured stone, and Saint-Denis-Basilique, commemorating the Royal Basilica of Saint-Denis. The number of stations with themes has greatly increased recently, and a selection of other stations with themes include:

Line 6   MONTPARNASSE-BIENVENÜE – Photographic section on eastbound platform showing development of Métro in honour of Fulgence Bienvenüe, the 'Father of the Métro'.

Line 13   VARENNE – This station is near to the Biron Mansion, in which is located the Rodin Museum, housing his sculptures. Replica statues can be seen on the southbound island platform, each piece being spotlit.

Line 2   VICTOR HUGO – Displays commemorating the work of this famous writer.

Line 3   PARMENTIER – An agricultural theme, with the potato given prominence.

Line 7b   BOLIVAR – A display about the work and life of Simon Bolivar.

Line 13   LIÈGE – Restored to Nord-Sud style, with murals relating to this Belgian city.

Line 10   CLUNY LA SORBONNE – Reopened in February 1988 after being closed for nearly forty years, the station has mosaic tiles on the vault depicting birds and signatures of famous names connected with Sorbonne University.

A magnificent example of a restored Nord-Sud station can be seen on line 13 at Liège which is unusual (like Commerce on line 8) in having its two platforms separated by a short section of tunnel, due to the narrow street configurations above. Liège, like Rennes on line 12, is open on Mondays to Saturdays only until 20.00. Brian Hardy

Line 12   ASSEMBLÉE NATIONALE – Renamed from Chambre des Députés in 1989. Large nameless silhouettes are the main theme on advert spaces in various colours, which illustrate the phrase above 'Wherever its members are gathered together, there is the National Assembly'. The work was completed in December 1990.

Line 5   PORTE DE PANTIN – Completed in November 1989, the station also gained the suffix 'Parc de la Villette'. The tiled walls comprise coloured musical 'note' symbols on a white background. The station ceiling in dark blue had a laser installed to show motifs. With the new style seating and diffused lighting, it is said to create the atmosphere of a music hall!

Line 7   PONT NEUF – Completed in December 1989 with the suffix 'La Monnaie', its theme is related to the Museum of the Mint opposite the station. Replica coins and medallions adorn the station vault.

Line 12   CONCORDE – What might seem an oversized 'Scrabble' board, the theme is an alphabetical puzzle on the Rights of Man and the Citizen. It goes without saying that the 44,000 ceramic tiles had to be carefully applied! Seats akin to those found in parks and city squares have been installed.

Line 7   CHAUSSÉE D'ANTIN – A large painting covers all of the vault which is dedicated to La Fayette, the French hero of the American War of Independence, whose name now appears as a suffix on the platforms of lines 7 and 9. The work was sponsored by the nearby and famous department store 'Galleries Lafayette', and was completed in November 1989.

Line 9   CHAUSSÉE D'ANTIN – The vault mural depicts common images of France and America – sciences, cinema, literature, poets and music. Additional lighting has been deflected upwards to illustrate the work.

There are several Métro stations which have been modernised commemorating special events or people. The platforms at Bastille on line 1 were completed in 1989 to commemorate the bi-centenary of the French Revolution. RATP

The ceilings of both lines 7 and 9 at Chaussée d'Antin (La Fayette) have been decorated with murals. On line 9, illustrated here, the theme depicts common images of France and America, and additional lighting has been installed to highlight the murals. RATP

In 1989 Chambre des Députés on line 12 was renamed Assemblée Nationale and in the following year was modernised, with large nameless silhouettes occupying the normal advert spaces. RATP

A section of the southbound platform on line 12 at Concorde showing the alphabetical puzzle with the theme on the Rights of Man and the Citizen. RATP

The four elevated stations on line 2 are very similar in design to each other, being very straight and having canopies to near the platform edge. This view at Stalingrad on 3 May 1992 looks west towards Porte Dauphine. Jeanne Gill

Quai de la Gare is typical of the elevated stations on line 6, in having an overall roof and mostly in unmodernised condition. Brian Hardy

A late evening view
of the entrance to
Saint François Xavier
on line 13, showing
illuminating Métro
signs on either side
of a concrete
stairwell.
Brian Hardy

It would be wrong to consider the stations of the Métro solely in terms of their interior design and to neglect one of their most characteristic features, the entrances. While the access stairways and passageways, constructed with due regard for economy, were undistinguished and, in many cases, very soon inadequate for the volume of traffic, the CMP, with some prompting from Charles Garnier, decided to make the entrances 'an object of beauty' and to this end organised a competition for their design. As far back as 1886, when it seemed likely that the long-discussed underground railway was about to be built, Garnier, the architect of the Paris Opéra, wrote to the then Minister of Public Works and urged that the Métro should shun all association with industry and turn instead to bronze and stone, marble and triumphal columns, adorned with sculptures. Nothing came of the 1886 project and the art form most closely associated with the Métro was one totally different from Garnier's classicism. None of the designs submitted – all very dependent on traditional ideas – pleased the directors of the CMP and their final choice was rejected by the municipality. The Chairman of the company, the banker Adrien Bernard, who was himself a great admirer of Art Nouveau, then had the inspired idea of awarding the commission to a relatively unknown young architect, Hector Guimard, who was only 32 at the time. Having qualified as an architect and won a travel scholarship, he did not follow the well-trodden path to Rome, but instead went off to Brussels, where he studied under Vincent Horta, the first European exponent of Art Nouveau. Working in forged iron, Guimard created balustrades in which curves and hollows flowed into each other without beginning or end and the letter 'M' was created by their meeting. The entrances were marked by two curving uprights, at the end of which were flower-like globes, illuminated at night. Between these was a plate with the name 'Métropolitain' in flowing letters and the signature of the architect. At the more important stations, the entrances were covered by pavilions in the same general style, but with variations, those at Bastille and Étoile being almost monumental, with a touch of the oriental.

Guimard was not without his critics, and as early as 1904 the CMP was persuaded to abandon the designs he had prepared for Opéra and to substitute rather pedestrian stone balustrades designed by Cassien Bernard. Nevertheless, some 87 Guimard entrances survive on lines 1 to 8, and in 1978 were given the protection of 'listed building' status.

An original Guimard glass canopy station entrance survives at one of the entrances at Porte Dauphine on line 2, as seen here in this tranquil setting. Another can be seen at Abbesses on line 12 but is not of Nord-Sud origin, instead originating from Hôtel de Ville. Jeanne Gill

There are plenty of the less ornate Guimard station entrances surviving in the style illustrated here at Palais Royal. This station name gained the appendage 'Musée du Louvre' in 1989 to indicate its close proximity to the Louvre museum. It is pleasing to note that the complete station name is in old style lettering, although being fairly new. Jeanne Gill

Two have also found their way into museums of modern art, in New York and Paris. The pavilions have fared less well and only Porte Dauphine on line 2 survives, blending quietly into the trees of the Bois de Boulogne. None of the canopies remain on their original site, but that from Hôtel de Ville was re-erected at Abbesses when displaced by the entry to an underground car park. While it adds character to the pretty little Montmartre square in which it stands, it is historically quite out of place, as the Nord-Sud at no time availed itself of Guimard's talents.

Apart from the stone balustrades mentioned above, Guimard's style gave way to a much more sombre design in wrought iron, designed by Dervaux. First used on the southern section of line 4, these entrances were generally used for all stations opened between the wars. They are marked by a column surmounted by a globe, illuminated at night. The Nord-Sud used a similar design, but with a more intricate design of balustrade. Reinforced concrete pavilions appeared on the extensions of the 1930s, generally used to provide cover for escalators.

Two examples of less usual Métro entrance signs are seen at Bastille (left), using a rather familiar bar-and-circle design! Bourse on line 3 (right) also has an unusual 'Metropolitain' sign at its entrance. Note the escalator which brings passengers from ticket hall to street level, there being many of these short-rise machines around the Métro system, this one being installed in 1974. Jeanne Gill

The modern Métro entrance sign is plain and simple as illustrated at the entrance to Esplanade de La Défense on 3 May 1992. A yellow 'M' says it all! Brian Hardy

Entrances constructed in recent years have used modern materials such as fibreglass and are generally much lighter and simpler than those of earlier days. Present-day escalators can be unprotected and many exit directly onto the street. A post with a yellow 'M' is a rather plain successor to the Guimard entrances.

Station ticket offices were originally very simple and not particularly inviting. Gradually these became more welcoming. Maps of the system appeared and in 1937 these were supplemented by illuminated journey planners. In 1946 maps of the surrounding area were first displayed (q.v. below) and gradually, where space permitted, other facilities such as news-stands, telephones, information booths and boutiques have been added to make available to passengers a wide range of services.

Within stations, directions are given with reference to the termini of a line – there is no need to carry a compass, but the visitor should memorise the names of the terminal stations! Intermediate stations are normally listed in the corridor or at the stairs giving access to a platform. These show the stations in line order, with interchanges on the right. On the platforms, exit signs are blue and 'correspondance' (interchange) indications, leading to other lines, are orange. If there is more than one exit, plaques on the wall helpfully indicate the names of the streets and the house numbers to which each gives access. Ticket halls and some platforms also have a very useful 'Plan du Quartier' which shows the streets and the more important public buildings in the area, and exactly where the station entrances are situated. As an experiment the first television screens on Métro platforms appeared on 23 December 1985 and by the end of December the following year 26 station platforms had been so equipped. A total of 49 station platforms were ultimately equipped, relaying news, information and commercial advertising, the TVs being either on pedestals or suspended from the ceilings. Known as 'Tube' the scheme did not attract advertisers and therefore did not meet its costs. The service terminated on 22 December 1989 and the screens were removed over the following two months.

Lifts

Although the original agreement of 1898 specified that the CMP should instal lifts where there was a difference of 12 metres or more between street and platform level, or between the platforms of two corresponding lines, the CMP at first regarded lifts as an expense to be avoided, and the first was not placed in service (at République) until November 1910. Several more lifts were provided for the deeper stations on lines 4 and 7, but at the outbreak of the war in 1914, only seven stations were so equipped. Several more were placed in service when line 10 was opened and the Nord-Sud company could not avoid the provision of lifts at the deeper stations on line 12. However, they have always been relatively uncommon on the Métro and some of the earlier installations have now been replaced by escalators.

The first lifts were hydraulic, but those for lines 4 and 7 were electrically-powered. An unsuccessful return to hydraulic power was made with the lifts for line 10 and these were replaced by escalators. The first automatic lifts were placed in service at Havre-Caumartin on line 9 in 1937 and after 1945 all older lifts were gradually replaced by new ones for this method of operation. The general rate of travel is 3.5m/second.

As at 1 January 1993 there were 26 lifts at eleven stations, the deepest being at Buttes-Chaumont on line 7bis (28.70m), while the shortest rise is at Saint-Michel on line 4 (8.08m). At certain stations, such as at Saint-Michel and Cité, the lifts take passengers directly to and from platform level.

In comparison with the vast number of escalators on the Métro, there are very few lifts. Here at Jaurès two single lifts take passengers between street level and the elevated platforms on line 2, this being to the Porte Dauphine (westbound) direction.
Brian Hardy

Escalators

While the average depth of Métro stations is not so great in comparison with those on London's tube lines, the development of escalators on the system was for many years a very slow process. Nevertheless, since the first practical escalator in the world was used at the Paris Exhibition in 1900, it is perhaps not surprising that escalators first appeared on the Métro before lifts did. The first escalator was installed at Père-Lachaise in 1909, but even by 1923 only eight machines were in service. These early escalators were rather slow (65 steps/minute) and all were of the shunt landing type with passengers having to step off sideways on leaving. They were thus awkward to use, especially for ladies in fashionable tight hobble-skirts.

Escalators of the modern comb type with wooden cleated treads had a speed of 90 steps/minute and were first used at Porte des Lilas in 1924. Again, development was slow and as late as 1966 there were only 87 in service at 50 stations. In general, escalators were installed only where the difference in height was over 4m and even then very often in the ascending direction only. In part, the use of escalators was held back by the automatic (portillon) gates, which closed off the platforms as trains arrived. As these very quickly led to the build-up of a crowd (when closed), escalators could only be used where there was enough space for this crowd to form without blocking off would-be travellers.

As with the control of tickets, it was the coming of the RER which altered matters. A programme drawn up in 1966 provided for the purchase of 200 new escalators, of which 34 were for the Métro. Since then the growth in the number of escalators has been phenomenal, with 415 in use at 196 stations at 1 June 1992, which excludes a further 284 in operation on the RATP's RER network. This development has been helped by the introduction in1973 of 'compact' escalators with a width overall of only 1.5m (as against the normal 1.7m) and an angle of incline of 35° as opposed to the usual 30°. These do not require to be protected from the weather and at many places, such as bus interchange stations, they lead directly into the open. The first of the weatherproof escalators was commissioned at Place Monge on line 7. Density of passenger flow rather than the depth of a station is now the main factor governing the installation of new escalators. It should be noted that many escalators on the Métro are controlled by photo-electric cells, and are set in motion by the approach of a passenger. If no others come along, the escalator stops again after sufficient time has elapsed for that passenger to have reached the top or bottom. The general speed of escalators on the Métro is now 100 steps/minute. The escalators with the greatest rise are at Places des Fêtes on line 7bis (22.45m), while the shortest are at Havre Caumartin on line 3 (2.60m). A total of 97 Métro escalators have a rise less than 4m.

The following list of lines and numbers of escalators (a total of 415 at 196 stations) is as of 1 June 1992. It should be pointed out, however, that in some cases the escalators for an interchange station may not necessarily be divided between all the lines served by it – for example, Saint-Lazare (lines 3, 12 and 13) has five serving line 3, ten serving line 13, but none allocated to line 12.

	Escalators	Stations		Escalators	Stations
Line 1	42	14	Line 7bis	6	3
Line 2	15	8	Line 8	33	21
Line 3	52	20	Line 9	43	23
Line 3bis	4	1	Line 10	8	7
Line 4	31	13	Line 11	11	7
Line 5	29	10	Line 12	23	17
Line 6	21	10	Line 13	34	15
Line 7	63	27			

Travolators

Despite the initial planning of the Métro system, it was not always possible to ensure that the distances at interchange stations were as short as the public might have wished and some of the corridors on the Métro are exceptionally long. The CMP had considered the idea of travolators in the 1930s, but had been unable to put the idea into practice beyond ensuring that the necessary width was left in some passageways of new construction. It was not until 1964 that the first pair of travolators were put into service on 21 October at Châtelet, linking lines 1 and 4 with 7 and 11. They were 131m long and 0.92m wide and a speed of 45m/minute (2.7 km/h) allowed them to carry 10,000 passengers per hour. In service they proved to be slightly too small and slow, and when the next set (of three) were installed at Montparnasse-Bienvenüe on 25 July 1968, they were made rather wider (1.12m) and had a speed of 3km/h, allowing a capacity of 11,000 passengers per hour. Two have also been installed at Invalides, connecting the Métro with RER line C, which is operated wholly by the SNCF. The total number of travolators on the Métro is thus seven, at three stations.

In 1992 there were 415 escalators serving the Métro system, the majority of them being of post 1967 origin. This pair at Porte d'Orléans were commissioned in June 1967, the first since 1961.
Brian Hardy

A view of the two travolators at Châtelet, linking Métro lines 1 and 4 with 7 and 11. A further three link the Métro with the RER in this extensive station complex.
Jeanne Gill

Station Names

When Baron Haussmann, Préfect of the Seine, drove 85 miles of new streets across Paris between 1855 and 1870, he obliterated many of the ancient villages, so that when the first line of the Métro opened in July 1900, there were few old villages to use for station names. Instead, the names of important buildings on the line of route were used, as well as the name of a Square (Place) or a street (rue), mostly at right-angles to the line. It seems that some of the names had the 'Place de' and 'Rue de' prefixes dropped before signs were installed at stations, apart from a few odd exceptions, which still survive (e.g. Place de Clichy and Rue Montmartre, which are to avoid confusion with Porte de Clichy and Boulevard de Montmartre respectively). With Métro stations spaced close together, names used had to be those of streets where the stations actually were. But as the system grew, the name of a street at right-angles to the first line could be parallel to the second line, for which it was clearly imprecise. In many cases, therefore, a second name was added for the interchange, but in others an entirely new name was used. At the ends of the lines, at the City boundaries, the prefix 'Porte' (Gate) was used on station names, and have been retained, even though the City fortifications had been dismantled by 1920.

Considering France's history, generals and battles of the Napoleons are well represented in station names. There are 18 generals and 5 battles associated with Napoleon I, 5 generals and 4 battles associated with Napoleon III and 7 generals and 9 battles for the rest of French history. Such examples are Cambronne (line 6), Daumesnil (6/8), Duroc (12/13), Kléber (6), Mouton-Duvernet (4) and Pelleport (3bis) – all generals, and Austerlitz (line 5), Pyramides (7), Iéna (9) and Wagram (3) – all battles of Napoleon I.

Double-barrelled names are not always of two streets at right-angles. There are innumerable combinations, but apart from double names in their own right, such as Buttes-Chaumont or Chardon-Lagache, these can be what is in effect one street at right-angles, but which changes its name as it crosses the line, or a street name combined with a square, or a square or bridge combined with a district, or two villages. As there is a flat fare on the Métro, and thus there is no need to ask for specific destination names when purchasing a ticket, passengers do not have to quote some very long names – e.g. 'Boulogne – Pont de Saint-Cloud – Rhin et Danube' on line 10, or 'Bobigny – Pablo Picasso – Préfecture Hôtel du Département' on line 5!

Name changes have, of course, taken place for various reasons. Apart from new lines which have caused name changes to interchange stations, the two world wars have also had their effects on Métro station names. For example, Berlin (Nord-Sud line B, now line 13) was closed in 1914 and later reopened as Liège. In the same year, Allemagne was swiftly renamed Jaurès, after a Socialist politician who had been assassinated in that year. During the First World War, Pont d'Austerlitz became Quai de la Rapée in 1916, and after that war Alma was renamed George V.

After the Second World War, Franklin D. Roosevelt gave his name to a station in 1946 and seven stations were renamed after heroes of the resistance, including the two Corentins (Celton and Cariou) and Colonel Fabien.

In 1942 there were three big changes to give double-barrelled names to stations which had been hitherto linked as interchanges, but under separate names. Montparnasse (line 4 and 12) and Bienvenüe (lines 6 and 14) became Montparnasse-Bienvenüe, which still survives, but the other two have been changed again to become Franklin D. Roosevelt and Stalingrad, both in 1946.

Some names have disappeared from the map, only to re-appear elsewhere at a later date. These include Rue Saint-Denis which became Réaumur-Sébastopol in 1907, the first year of any name changes on the Métro, but was used in Boulevard Saint-Denis opened on line 4 in 1908, and by line 13 reaching the actual town of Saint-Denis in 1976. Austerlitz, disappearing in 1916, re-appeared as Gare d'Orléans-Austerlitz in 1930. Today, it is just plain Gare d'Austerlitz, even though the destinations of some trains on line 10 still refer to the previous name, from which it was renamed in 1977. Already mentioned is that Alma became George V in 1920, but Alma-Marceau opened in 1923. Torcy became Marx Dormoy in 1946, but re-appeared as a New Town at the end of the new branch on RER line A in 1980. Line 4's station at Vaugirard was renamed Saint Placide in 1913, three years after the Nord-Sud company's Vaugirard station with the same name was opened – and remains so named to this day. In addition, the name Sèvres appears twice on the Métro – in Pont de Sèvres (line 9) and Sèvres-Babylone (lines 10 and 12).

Since 1970 there have been ten alterations to station names on the Métro, some of them only in the form of suffixes added. Summarised, these are:

Year	Line(s)	Old Name	New Name
1970	2	Bagnolet	ALEXANDRE DUMAS
1970	1–2–6	Étoile	CHARLES DE GAULLE – ÉTOILE
1986	9	Nation	NATION – PLACE DES ANTILLES
1989	1–7	Palais Royal	PALAIS ROYAL – MUSÉE DU LOUVRE
1989	1	Louvre	LOUVRE-RIVOLI
1989	12	Chambre des Députés	ASSEMBLÉE NATIONALE
1989	5	Porte de Pantin	PORTE DE PANTIN – PARC DE LA VILLETTE
1989	7	Porte de la Villette	PORTE DE LA VILLETTE – CITÉ DES SCIENCES ET DE L'INDUSTRIE
1989	7–9	Chaussée d'Antin	CHAUSSÉE D'ANTIN – LA FAYETTE
1989	7	Pont Neuf	PONT NEUF – LA MONNAIE

In addition to all the main station names, there are many which have suffixes in their own right. For example, Javel - André Citroën (the latter in respect of the famous car manufacturer) and Porte d'Orléans - Général Leclerc, the suffix honouring the famous Free French General, who entered Paris at the head of his armoured division, and liberated Strasbourg. He was posthumously promoted 'Marshal' in 1952, so that the street and station names are technically incorrect. Another World War II hero is honoured in Porte Dauphine - Maréchal de Lattre de Tassigny.

CHAPTER FOUR
ROLLING STOCK

The original rolling stock of the CMP had a distinct affinity with contemporary tramcars. The wooden-bodied cars were about 8m long and carried at most 50 passengers. They rode on four-wheel trucks and had two 125 hp motors. Air brakes were used. For their size they were very heavy, the motor coaches weighing 18.5 tonnes and the trailers 8.5 tonnes. Two single-width sliding doors were originally provided on each side, one for entry and one for exit, but in a very short time these were seen to be inadequate, and after 1902 new deliveries had double-width doors, the earlier cars being converted to this design. Twelve of the original motor coaches were double-ended but the majority had only one driving cab. Because of the events related below, the two-axle motors had a very short life and all had been withdrawn by 1906. The trailers were in some cases rebuilt as bogie motors but others survived unaltered on lines 2 and 6 until 1932.

The first trains on line 1 consisted of a motor coach pulling two trailers, but this formation very soon became insufficient to cope with the traffic and in 1901 it was decided to strengthen these and to operate trains of seven or eight coaches on line 2. As multiple unit traction was then in its infancy, there was no certainty that it would be able to cope with the demands of everyday traffic on the Métro and it was therefore decided to adopt the Thomson 'double traction' system, which had been devised in 1898 and which, though somewhat limited in its ultimate potential, was both simple and robust. Current collection and control was by the leading motor coach. Current was passed through a huge controller to the motors of both the leading and another motor coach at line voltage by a bus line and, as the CMP placed the second motor at the rear on lines without terminal loops, this line ran the length of the train. When accelerating, resistances were not cut out progressively as in normal systems, but were instead brought in in parallel with the resistance on the previous notch of the controller and it was not possible to bridge the gap from series to parallel operation without briefly cutting off the current. This manœuvre demanded care on the part of the driver, since the slightest backward movement of the controller could produce arcing. The equipment was protected by circuit breakers, not seen again on the Métro until the advent of the articulated stock (MA52) in 1952. The power-weight ratio on an eight-coach train was very low (500hp to approximately 110 tonnes with a full load) and the little motor coaches were often seen to be labouring on the ramps leading to the elevated sections of line 2. But the double-traction trains had solved the capacity problem and an order for 284 additional vehicles was placed in 1903.

On 10 August 1903 a short-circuit caused a fire to break out in the leading motor coach of a double-traction train at Boulevard Barbès station just at the end of the evening rush hour. The staff on the spot decided to push the train to the siding at Belleville by using the following four-coach train, both trains being emptied of their exasperated passengers. Despite warnings by large clouds of black smoke issuing from the disabled motor, the convoy set off. Unfortunately the points at Belleville had not been set for the siding and it was decided to press on to the terminus at Nation, the train by now being in tunnel. It had reached Ménilmontant when fire broke out with terrible strength. At that moment, the following very crowded train stopped in Couronnes, the preceding station, and the Station Master, with great promptitude, asked the passengers to evacuate the train, but the majority stayed put until the cloud of smoke issued from the tunnel mouth and all the lights went out. Loss of life was considerable – 84 passengers perished in this disaster. Not only the CMP, but underground railways generally, learned much from it.

There were many factors contributing to the disaster, but the immediate blame was placed on the underpowered, wooden motor coaches and the order just placed was cancelled. As a temporary measure, the maximum train length was reduced to seven coaches, with the two motors placed together at the head, but as soon as was practicable they were withdrawn for conversion to bogie stock, the last running on 14 May 1906.

The original CMP stock had wooden bodies, but from 1903-04 metal equipment compartments painted brown had become standard. M305 is preserved in the transport museum at Saint-Mandé.
Brian Hardy

An olive green livery soon followed as shown on this preserved example of a two-motored (M2) motor car M535 in the Paris Transport Museum. Note that the passenger doors are still wooden.
Julian Pepinster

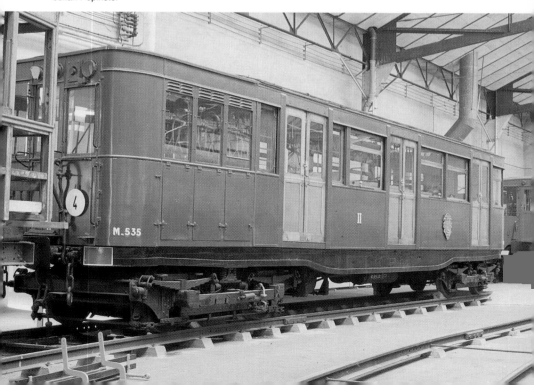

The Classic Stock

The history of the Classic, Sprague, stock is extremely complicated and as it is almost extinct, no more than a summary can be attempted here.

The first two prototype bogie motor coaches were delivered in December 1902 and April 1903 and were numbered 1001 and 1002. They had wooden bodies but the driving compartments and switchgear were encased in metal. They worked as a double-traction unit and spent all of their lives on line 2, later being renumbered 301/2. Briefly in 1914-15 they were re-equipped with four motors, but the experiment was not successful and they were re-converted to two-motor condition. These vehicles, however, set the general standard of appearance for all stock built up to 1937.

Even before the Couronnes fire, the CMP seemed to have been considering the use of multiple-unit control, probably recognising that the double-traction equipment could only be a stop-gap. An eight-coach train, with three two-axle motor coaches working in multiple-unit, appeared on line 1 early in November 1903, and so anxious was the CMP to see how it would perform, that it was apparently placed in service before official permission to use it had been given. This train used the Sprague system, one of three then available. Wisely, the CMP spent much time and money evaluating the various systems, both singly and in combination, before finally deciding in 1908 on the Sprague-Thomson system. It was an excellent choice and was to give superb service for 75 years, standing up uncomplainingly to the overcrowding and minimal maintenance of the years of the second world war.

The Sprague system of multiple unit operation, already in use on the Chemin de Fer de l'Ouest, consisted of an electro-magnetic reverser and a pilot-motor-operated drum controller. Current relays gave automatic acceleration and only five control wires were used. The system was essentially simple and easy to maintain, but it tended to be imprecise and jerky in operation, especially in the transition from series to parallel.

The Westinghouse system was electro-pneumatic, using a control line of seven wires and contactors. It required frequent and careful maintenance and even then it was not always possible to ensure that the same amount of current reached each motor at the same time. Acceleration was slow and, with an inexperienced driver, could be jerky. By the 1920s, when the 100 Westinghouse motors were concentrated on line 4, the equipment was wearing out and chaos often ensued when second-time exasperated passengers abandoned trains which had stalled on the climb to Gare du Nord, making it necessary to cut off the current to prevent a major tragedy. By the time normality was restored in the late evening, trains were completely out of order and the railway management in despair! The Westinghouse trains were withdrawn in 1929/30 and converted to Sprague-Thomson equipment. This conversion would have taken place earlier if finance had been available. The problems caused by the Westinghouse trains put the CMP off anything electro-pneumatic until the advent of the rubber-tyred trains in the 1950s.

Of the three systems available, the Thomson control proved to be the best. It allowed both hand notching or automatic acceleration, the latter being activated by the handle of the master controller through a spring-operated drum. It gave precise control of each motor in a train (though all worked at the pace of the weakest), it was easy to maintain and it was reliable. The main drawback was that the control line required nine wires and it was impossible to add supplementary notches to the complex and rather delicate control mechanism. It had reached the limit of its development, and was fitted to 271 coaches.

Having experimented and gained some experience of each of these forms of control, the CMP decided to adopt a combination of the Sprague and Thomson systems. In this Sprague-Thomson system, a small master controller energised one or more of a small number of train wires commanding self-contained automatic electro-magnetic contactor equipment. This gave easy and smooth control of acceleration and also allowed the grouping of motors so that failure of one did not incapacitate an entire train. Following experiments, the first trains so equipped were placed in service in 1908. From then until the 1930s, the Sprague-Thomson system gradually replaced all other forms of control and gave the CMP a secure and reliable fleet, with a degree of standardisation not enjoyed by any other operator before or since. The only later exception was a batch of 21 motor coaches with Jeumont-Heidmann equipment delivered in 1930. Although this gave excellent results on the gradients of line 3, the interest of standardisation prevailed and no more such equipment was purchased for the Métro. These trains could not be worked with Sprague-Thomson stock. This type of equipment was later used on the Chemin de Fer d'Orléans stock, more familiarly known as the Z stock of the Ligne de Sceaux.

Following the successful operation of the prototypes and as a result of the Couronnes fire, the CMP placed 177 motor bogie coaches in service in 1904 and 1905. Before they entered service, however, the train of four-wheelers fitted with Sprague multiple unit equipment had been tried in November 1903 on line 1. The bogie coaches carried these experiments a stage further. They were of two lengths; the 300 class were only 10.85m long and had two doors per side, while the 400 class had an additional area for standing passengers immediately behind the compartment housing the equipment. Some of the former had double-traction control and went to line 2, but the majority were fitted for multiple-unit operation and went to line 1. All the 400 class were m.u. fitted and were placed in service on line 3. All the 300 class m.u. motor cars were lengthened in 1910 to make them identical with the 400 class and both of these classes received four motors in 1929-32, surviving unchanged until withdrawal from the late-1960s and into the 1970s. The double traction members of the 300 class were withdrawn in 1931 and many of the parts were used in the building of new four-motor coaches.

The next series to appear were 114 rebuilds of four-wheel motors, those with Westinghouse equipment being fitted for multiple unit operation, using the products of the same manufacturer, while the double-traction coaches retained this equipment. As rebuilt, they were identical to the 300 class. In 1906-07, 56 two-axle cars were similarly rebuilt and finally another batch of 24 were built new. This last batch were the first coaches on the Métro to have all-metal bodywork. The majority of these coaches were lengthened in 1909-12 so that they also resembled the 400 class and a large number were further rebuilt with four motors between 1929 and 1936, in the course of which operation the remaining wooden bodies were replaced by metal ones. Those built for service on line 1 were in grey livery.

The next batch of new coaches, the 500s, reverted to the longer length of the 400 class, but had all-metal bodywork. Their history was much less complicated since they were not rebuilt in any way and the class survived intact until after 1967. These were the first to have Sprague-Thomson equipment and so may be regarded as the definitive version of the Classic stock. They were followed in 1909 by the broadly similar 600 class which, however, originally had Thomson equipment, and in 1913-14 by the 700 class, which had Sprague-Thomson and incorporated various minor improvements. The last of these were intended for line 6 and would have had two driving cabs, but because of the German advance into northern France in 1914 they were never built.

The motor coaches delivered after the First World War were characterised by a much smaller switchgear compartment, with a consequent enlargement of the passenger area. This series appeared between 1921 and 1927 and the last 18 were double-ended for use on line 10 and the shuttle (Navette).

To improve service speeds on the busier lines, it was decided in 1925 to introduce four-motored motor coaches of a slightly greater length. The first batch of 62, 14.2m long, had three pairs of doors per side and went into service in 1927-28, mostly on line 3, but some migrated to line 12 after the merger of the Nord-Sud company with the CMP. Of the later deliveries, all were of the same length and all had four pairs of double doors per side. About half were built new and the rest were rebuilds of earlier stock (q.v. above). Ten of the new coaches were in grey livery. The four-motor stock could always be distinguished by a small signalling window to the right of the driving cab. The last batches of four-motor cars had the arrangement of the doors and windows equally spaced on each side.

The Nord-Sud motor coaches did not differ greatly from their contemporaries on the CMP and although built over the period 1909-25, were all visually identical to each other. They were slightly larger in profile and heavier than the Métro stock and had a much improved design of bogie. As they had less powerful motors, their progress was comfortable and stately rather than lively! Apart from one coach scrapped as a result of an

A recent addition to the Railway Museum in Mulhouse is Sprague M4 motor car M1354. A motor coach of Z stock from the Ligne de Sceaux (now RER line B) can be seen in the background.
Fred Ivey

Also preserved in the Paris Transport Museum is an M4 from the Nord-Sud Company — now lines 12 and 13. A two-tone blue livery was carried on these cars, although first class cars were cream with red ends.
Brian Hardy

accident just after the Nord-Sud merger with the CMP, all were incorporated into CMP stock in 1930. One coach was damaged by bombing in 1944 and, with eight others, was rebuilt for works train duties in 1952, but all the others survived in service until 1971-72. The increase in line voltage was the main reason for their rather sudden demise.

The first bogie trailer cars were delivered with the 400 class motors, which they closely resembled, though the first class vehicles were panelled in metal and were thus the first coaches on the Métro to be painted rather than varnished. The next batch were shorter and were intended to make up, with corresponding motors, six-coach trains on line 1. They later went to other lines and when withdrawn in 1935 three were sold to the Brussels-Tervuren Electric Railway, for which they had to be re-gauged. This is the only case of Métro stock being sold for further service on urban railways elsewhere. These were followed in the period 1908-13 by a large number of trailers based on the 500 class motors. After the First World War came two batches of trailers 13.60m long of which eight, fitted with Brill diamond bogies, were by far the most comfortable of all Métro coaches. Unfortunately the experiment was not repeated. Finally, there were five lots of four-door trailers, corresponding to the four-motor motor coaches. Many of these were painted grey for line 1 and in these rather more attention was paid to detail than was generally the case. The last batch had lightweight aluminium bodies and a new design of bogie, and weighed only 15.2 tonnes.

The interior of the Sprague stock was rather basic, having wooden seats, windows that opened on one side only and open lantern roofs. The first class cars had hard leather seating. Brian Hardy

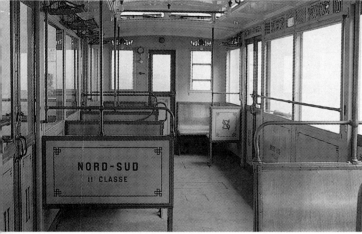

For comparison, an interior view of a second class Nord-Sud car. Julian Pepinster

The Nord-Sud trailers resembled very closely that system's motor cars, but were fitted with rectangular end windows.

The interior of all varieties of the Classic stock was simple to the point of austerity. The seats in the second class were of painted or varnished wood, while the first class boasted leather upholstery, but without a great deal of padding. Lighting was by three strings of $5 \times 40W$ lamps and ventilation was provided by drop windows (on one side of the coach only, to prevent cross-draughts) and by wide open vents in the lantern roof. Some of the last coaches to be built also had ventilators at foot level and travel on these on the open section of lines 2 and 6 in winter was guaranteed to chill even the most devoted rail fan, let alone the ordinary passengers. Neither heating nor sound insulation was provided and the train noises were thus most enjoyable for the enthusiast, though probably less so for the uninitiated. The floors, of corrugated sheet steel, were covered with magnesium cement.

The driving cabs were simply equipped, the driver sitting (but more often standing) on the right, working the controller with his right hand and the air brake valve with his left. The only instrument provided was the air-brake pressure gauge and speed had to be estimated. Glazed doors and panels gave the passenger a good view of all this, as well as of the fireworks from the traction-line switches, which were mounted, without any covering, to the left of the cab. There was no deadman's handle, but the master controller sprang back to 'off' if released and could not be moved away from that position unless the button in the centre of the handle was first depressed. In any case, the guard travelled in the leading coach at the leading pair of doors and was within sight of the driver.

The bogies were of 2.25m wheelbase and were of two types. Those built before 1912 had simple springing while the newer ones had a swing bolster. In neither case was the ride especially comfortable. Trailer bogies were of 1.8m wheelbase. The Westinghouse air brake was unsophisticated, with one cylinder per coach acting on one or two brake blocks per wheel. To prevent the deposition of metallic dust in the tunnels the brake blocks were of copper beech drenched in vegetable oil, giving off the typical Sprague era 'perfume'. The compressors were situated under the floor on motor coaches.

The Classic stock not only set the visual aspect of the Métro for many years, it also brought many unique sounds and smells, and the system no longer seems the same without it!

The original livery of the Classic stock was varnished wood and when the first all-metal coaches appeared, they were painted dark brown to match. Later, this was changed to a dark ('olive') green and in the 1920s this was in turn replaced by a medium green. The grey stock for line 1 was officially grey-blue, but the blue generally had to be imagined, as it faded very quickly. Many of the rebuilt coaches still incorporated the brown wooden doors of the original stock. The Nord-Sud stock was a pleasing shade of royal blue, with the first class trailers being cream with red ends. The CMP first class trailers were at first denoted by two white boards carried below the waist rail, but when the green livery was adopted for second class, first class trailers became red.

By 1937, therefore, the CMP had at its disposal a highly-standardised fleet. Apart from the coaches with J-H equipment, all stock had identical control, although the ex-Nord-Sud stock could not be coupled in multiple with the CMP stock. This standardisation and the rugged simplicity of the Classic stock were a godsend to both the maintenance and traffic staff during the difficult war years, when the Métro had to cope with unprecedented loads, but in time these very virtues became a drawback. As the standards of public expectation rose in the post-war period, the Métro began to seem noisy, uncomfortable and antiquated – it did not help that the trains built as recently as 1937 were really themselves based on designs dating back to 1903! The few experiments that were made, such as those with fluorescent lighting and regenerative braking, were isolated examples, intended to try out new ideas for the next generation of rolling stock, rather than to improve the Classic stock itself.

By any standards, the Classic stock of the Métro had an extraordinarily long career, spanning as it did the 79 years 1904–1983. Apart from two cars destroyed in the war (M33 and Bb619), systematic withdrawal of the Classic stock began only with the conversion of line 1 to 'pneu' operation, but even then many trains were transferred to reinforce other lines rather than being sent to the scrapyard. It was only when the MF67 stock began to arrive that serious inroads were made in the ranks of Sprague trains, which disappeared from lines 3 and 7 in 1971 and 1973 respectively. Some of these trains in due course turned up to replace the Nord-Sud stock on line 12. The extension of line 8 also created a need for many more trains and gave the Sprague stock a chance to show its paces on the Créteil line, where the stations are more widely spaced than elsewhere. In the 1970s, Sprague stock gave way to 'pneu' trains on line 6 in 1974 and to the articulated stock on line 10 (1975-76), while the last of the two-motor coaches went from line 2 (being replaced by four-motor coaches) in 1976. With the arrival of the MF77 stock, and by transfers of other modern stock, the Sprague stock disappeared from lines 5, 7bis, 8 and 12 in 1980, and from lines 2 and 3bis in 1981. By 1982, only 16 trains remained at work on line 9. These would have gone in September, but the flooding at Église de Pantin on 6 June 1982 and the subsequent temporary withdrawal of 18 MF67 trains granted a stay of execution, so that the last Sprague trains were finally withdrawn in April 1983.

However, they did not simply fade away. The Parisians had by now realised that a part of their city's history was about to pass away and the RATP commemorated the event with a ceremony never before accorded to any underground train. Under the general title of 'Salut l'Artiste', a series of events took place between 11 and 16 April 1983. At Miromesnil

From the late 1920s, the livery on Sprague stock cars was changed to bright green. The M4 motor cars were recognisable by having a small signal observation window to the right of the driver as seen on a train in its closing days of line 2 service. Brian Hardy

The livery of first class trailers was bright red, as illustrated by Ab487 entering Boulogne depot on line 9 whilst operating one of three RATP farewell special runs on 15 April 1983. Brian Hardy

In addition to cars of Sprague stock in bright green livery, there were also some cars in grey livery. These operated on line 1 until their replacement by rubber-tyred trains in 1963-64. They then went on lines 2, 8, 9 and 12 until scrapped and one set survived to run in the farewell celebrations, as seen at Porte de Montreuil on 15 April 1983. Brian Hardy

station there were, on successive days, a film show, a children's party, a mannequin parade and a concert, all in addition to a computer display. Saint-Augustin station hosted an exhibition on 'Art and the Métro' on the wide eastbound platform, while a rake of Sprague stock was stationed in the bay platform at Concorde on line 8, some of the carriages converted into a boutique selling souvenirs. Meanwhile, four Sprague trains (three of them decorated with special themes) ran to a published timetable on line 9 in the midday period, to cater for those who wanted a last ride. On Friday 15 April there was the official RATP farewell, when three trains carried official dignitaries from Porte de Montreuil to Pont de Sèvres and into Boulogne depot. After 79 years, therefore, it was (almost) over, with the very last public runs taking place on Saturday 16 April.

There are still three operational trains of Sprague stock which are used for filming, rail tours and special events. As they may operate on conventional lines, or (as illustrated here) on rubber-tyred lines, they have to be fitted with both types of shoegear.

As well as trains kept for special events, the Sprague stock lives on elsewhere in other ways. In the South of France at Cap d'Agde, near the harbour, there are some seats from withdrawn Sprague cars in the restaurant 'La Petite École', including the backs with decorative enamel panelling. For Sprague nostalgia, a visit here is a must — the food is excellent too!
Jeanne Gill

In fact, the last trains with the official party did not mark the end of the Sprague stock, which, in one form or another, will be around for some time yet. There are, for example, museum pieces which, until 1992, resided in the Paris Transport Museum at Saint Mandé. These, along with some others stored at various locations on the Métro system, will be housed in a new headquarters building for the RATP. Authorised on 28 February 1992, it will be located at Bercy between Quai de la Rapée and Gare de Lyon on the banks of the River Seine, close to the site of the Métro headquarters until the mid-1970s. When opened, these vehicles, along with some others from store, will once again be available for viewing as well as other examples of past Paris transport – buses, trams, trolleybuses, horse buses, a car from the funiculaire, horse cab and motor taxis.

The depot for engineers trains is located at Villette at the northern end of line 7, where this night-time view sees some former Sprague motor cars which have been converted into double-ended Tracteurs. Julian Pepinster

An engineers train with Tracteur T72 (formerly M628 and M629) nearest to the camera is seen at Porte de Clignancourt whose platforms were undergoing modernisation in 1992. Julian Pepinster

An interior of a Tracteur with the equipment (left) and the rather primitive driving controls. The Tracteur at the opposite end of this engineers' train can be seen through the open cab door.
Julian Pepinster

Former Sprague second class trailer Bb746 in its new role as VX5 seen in Boulogne depot in later MF67 stock livery.
Julian Pepinster

There are, of course, many other coaches of Sprague stock surviving elsewhere, both in the French provinces and abroad. Perhaps pride of place must go to four-motored motor car M1354 which can now be found in the railway museum at Mulhouse. Three complete operational trains have been retained by the RATP for use in film making and on enthusiasts' specials – Sprague stock has starred in many films, as in a hair-raising scene in 'Diva', where the young hero rides his motor scooter down a stairway and into a Sprague train!

There were numerous batches of Sprague stock, of all types of cars, each one ultimately representing one small piece of a very large jigsaw puzzle. Many different car builders were involved over the years in making the Classic stock, which, at its maximum in 1937, amounted to 2,720 cars, summarised as follows:

Driving Motor Cars ('M')	CMP M4 (Rebuilds)	340	
	CMP M4 (New Cars)	257	
	CMP M2	626	
	NS M4	114	1337
First Class Trailers ('Ab')	CMP	348	
	NS	51	399
Second Class Trailers ('Bb')	CMP	682	
	NS	100	782
Composite Trailers ('AB')	CMP	202	202
			2720

Remaining Sprague Stock as at 1 January 1993

Operative Train Sets:

M1308—Bb713—Ab411—Bb782—M429
M1266—Bb434—Ab475—Bb761—M1350
M103 —Bb751—Ab487—Bb572—M333

Other cars:

M2	M4	Ab	Bb	AB
M517	M270	Ab167	Bb171	AB5338
M757	M450	Ab253	Bb240	
M857	M473	Ab284	Bb453	
M1079	M1231	Ab464	Bb546	
	M1269	Ab1036*	Bb691	
	M1322	Ab1037*		
	M2103*			
	M2104*			

* Nord-Sud stock.

Other Sprague stock survivors had less glamorous roles. Many have been converted to 'Tracteurs' (motor cars for engineering trains), the majority of post-war conversions being double-ended, two motor coaches (less their trailing ends) making one Tracteur. Early works motor cars included the double-ended wooden four-wheel motors (MM1–12) displaced from passenger train duties in 1906 but surviving until 1949. Early conversions began in 1922 with T1 and T2 (ex-M313 and M316), followed by another 29 converted in the period 1928–37. The last conversions were undertaken in 1972. Similarly, many trailers have been converted over the years into wagons of various types, performing diverse roles, which bear the prefix 'V' or 'VX', while some ex-trailers retain their upper bodywork, being used as Personnel Carriers for works train staff. In addition there are a small number of 'Tracteurs Ateliers' (depot motor cars) and, like the works train Tracteurs, are fitted with both conventional and 'pneu' system shoegear, to enable them to work over all lines. A total of 14 new battery locomotives, built by Alsthom, were delivered in 1985–86, enabling some engineers trains to work 'on current' or on battery power.

The following works train vehicles were available as at 1 January 1993:

Tracteurs 'T'	70		Non-bogie wagons 'V'	6
Tracteurs Ateliers 'TA'	7		Special vehicles 'VX'	4
Battery locomotives 'TMA'	14		Plasser machine	1
Bogie vehicles/wagons 'V'	156			

Some trains of articulated MA52 stock can still be seen at work on line 10, although their days are numbered and look the worse for wear, as seen at Gare d'Austerlitz. David Rowe

The Articulated (MA52) Stock

After the end of the Second World War, studies were instituted for new rolling stock which, by virtue of improved acceleration and braking, would improve overall service speed and thus increase line capacity. These studies ultimately resulted in the articulated trains, the first of which arrived in September 1951 and went into service on line 13 in February 1952. The impending extension of this line from Porte de Saint-Ouen to Carrefour Pleyel (opened on 30 June 1952) made an increase in line capacity imperative.

The car bodies were built by Brissonneau et Lotz and each semi-permanently coupled unit consists of three car bodies resting on four bogies. The outer cars of a unit are 12.70m long and the middle trailer is shorter, at 9.70m. The outer (motor) cars were second class only, while the middle car was a composite. These trains introduced a new colour scheme of light blue and grey for second class and cream with blue lining for first class. Internally, the new stock represented a great step forward, having upholstered seating in both classes, fluorescent lighting and, improved ventilation. Each unit has four self-ventilated motors of 92hp controlled by type JH servo-motor-operated cam-contactor controllers. The bogies are of welded construction and incorporate 'Athermos' axle boxes with radial movement. Most of the bogies were constructed by Alsthom, but in three units by BL (E036, 039 and 040). On the articulated parts, rubber 'Silentblocs' are used. Braking is by Westinghouse air brakes and brake release is done electro-pneumatically under the control of a decelerometer, to give adequate retardation without wheelslip. The trains are fitted with Scharfenberg automatic couplers at the driving ends, but are semi-permanently coupled within units.

A start has already been made on scrapping a few of the MA52 trains. Unit E037 awaits its fate at Villette depot, standing alongside Tracteurs and Battery Locomotives — TMA. Pascal Lesure

An interior view of an articulated MA52 motor car. When this stock was refurbished for service on line 10 in 1975-76, additional lighting was fitted, along with tip-up seats by the doors. Brian Hardy

In service, the MA52 stock did much of what was expected of it, especially with regard to acceleration, but it was noisy and rough riding and the design was not repeated. Nevertheless, these trains have given sound service for over 35 years, at first on line 13, and since 1975-76 on line 10. Their interior furnishings set a standard which lasted until the MF77 stock appeared.

With line 13 being a 'Y'-shaped line, the articulated MA52 stock was ideal for uncoupling and operating short (one-unit) trains in service at certain off peak times. However, uncoupling ceased in 1972, not only with the stock's imminent transfer to line 10, but also to eliminate the operating problems associated with uncoupling and the extra staff needed for it.

Although given unit numbers, the articulated stock also has individual car numbers, driving motors prefixed 'D' and the shorter middle trailers prefixed 'C', as follows:

Unit	Formation
E001	D01 – C01 – D02
E002	D03 – C02 – D04
and so on, up to:	
E040	D79 – C40 – D80

For service on line 10, the opportunity was taken to modernise the 40 units of the MA52 fleet. A prototype conversion was undertaken at Vaugirard depot from August 1974, being completed in March 1975, unit E030 being the chosen one. The work involved utilising noise-reducing materials, increasing the fluorescent lighting, and installing tip-up seats at all door positions. The exteriors were repainted in a royal blue and white livery with a dark blue waistband, the first class section being denoted by a yellow band at cantrail height. The modernisation work on the other 39 units was undertaken at Saint Ouen depot, following deliveries of new MF67 stock to line 9, which reduced the amount of work to be done at that depot on the old Classic stock. The work on the MA52 stock was also to improve its reliability, and to give it a new lease of life. It was completed by the autumn of 1976 and allowed the replacement of the 1926–36 Sprague stock on line 10. At the same time, a small number of five-car trains of MF67 stock were allocated to line 10, as the 20 trains of MA52 stock alone were insufficient to provide the complete service on that line.

On the modernised MA52 stock, the position of the first class accommodation was also altered, as on line 10 the units would not be required to uncouple, and the first class was thus moved to the standard position in the middle of the train. This was achieved by converting one motor car of half of the 40 units and ensuring that they were always formed in the middle of a train. The odd-numbered motor car of each odd-numbered unit was selected for first class accommodation and therefore each train comprises one odd and one even-numbered unit. With semi-permanent train formations, the middle driving cabs became redundant, only equipment needed for shunting being retained (and locked away out of use when in service, so that the area could be used by passengers). The traffic levels, and as a result, service intervals, on line 10 do not warrant the investment of Automatic Train Operation, and thus the MA52 stock operates in conventional driving mode, but one-person-operated.

The MA52 stock, now 40 years old, is approaching the end of its working life and indeed, some units have already been withdrawn. The first withdrawals occurred in July 1987 and to date the operative fleet has been reduced to 13 trains. Of the withdrawn units, E015 and E016 have been utilised for experimental purposes (AIMT) on the former shuttle line at Porte des Lilas, while one car from E001 is now at the RATP's Technical School.

The remainder will be withdrawn when the new MF88 stock enters service on line 7bis, which will allow more MF67 stock to be transferred to line 10.

For the enthusiast, the articulated stock is well worth a visit, with its quite musical qualities and Westinghouse air brakes. The RATP deserves every credit for experimenting with articulation at a time (in the early 1950s) when it was not as fashionable in urban transport as it is now.

The experimental rubber-tyred car MP51 is seen here in the Paris Transport Museum standing on 'pneu' trackwork. Brian Hardy

The 'Pneu' Stock

The need for greater line capacity than could be obtained with conventional stock, and the great expense of lengthening stations to allow longer trains to be operated, caused a novel alternative to be considered by the RATP. Greater line capacity was to be obtained with the aid of the high acceleration and retardation given by the use of rubber tyres, and higher maximum speeds between closely spaced stations could be given by the same means. Extra comfort and lightweight vehicles would also be obtained.

Plans were thus formulated for experiments with rubber-tyred train operation. The 767m long 'shuttle' line between Porte des Lilas and Pré-Saint-Gervais was chosen, which had been closed to passengers since September 1939, and a special single car was built in 1951 by a consortium of manufacturers, with two 130hp Alsthom motors and Jeumont equipment. The motors were hung from the body, instead of being mounted on the bogies in the usual way, and drove the axles by cardan drive. A small pantograph, not normally visible, was fitted for shunting purposes. For the first time, rheostatic braking was fitted, backed up by electro-pneumatic brakes, with automatic deceleration and braking for normal service. The coach was classified 'MP51' and carried the stock number of 151 at each end. It was delivered on 25 July 1951 and was made available for inspection by the press and the public on 12 and 14 November 1951. The coach underwent exhaustive tests and trials and entered service on 13 April 1952 carrying passengers between 13.30 and 19.30 on the shuttle line. The trials also included experiments with Automatic Train Operation. The car was withdrawn from service on 31 May 1956 and, being an experiment, the service was not replaced. The car was put into store in 1961 and in April 1981 was taken to the Paris Transport Museum at Saint Mandé where it was put on display to the public, representing a very important stage in the transition of Paris Métro rolling stock.

For rubber-tyred train operation, the track has to be specially converted. It consists of conventional steel rails, which are retained as 'safety' rails, flanked by longitudinal bearing strips for the rubber tyred wheels, at 1.98m gauge. These strips were of tropical hardwood (now replaced), of reinforced concrete, or of wide metal 'T' beams. Vertical guide bars, which are also the conductor rails, are arranged 2.44m apart on insulating supports.

The bogies have rubber-tyred carrying wheels with tyres 1m in diameter, inflated to $9kg/cm^2$ (motor) or $6.5kg/cm^2$ (trailers). Inside there are conventional steel wheels with deep flanges which drop onto the safety rail if a tyre becomes deflated. Braking is by oiled-wood blocks onto these wheels. Shoes rubbing on the safety rails give both negative return and track circuit operation for automatic signalling. Spring-loaded shoes press sideways onto the guide bars for current collection. Guide wheels on vertical axles fit between the guide bars – their tyres are 0.54m diameter, inflated to $9kg/cm^2$.

At points and crossings, the longitudinals are lowered to the level of the steel rails and the guide rails interrupted; the deep flanges of the steel wheels then guide the train. Severe speed limits are in force at these locations.

From these experiments it was decided that the idea of rubber-tyred train operation on the Métro was sound and the whole of line 11 was chosen for conversion to 'pneu' operation. Although a relatively short line, 6.287km from Châtelet to Mairie des Lilas, it nevertheless had a wide variety of technical problems to offer, such as many curves and an almost continuous gradient at 1 in 25. The new stock for line 11 was formed into four-car sets formed of two driving motor cars (M), one non-driving motor car (N) and one composite trailer (AB), in the formation M – N – AB – M. Known as the **MP55** type, it was built in two separate batches, as follows:

Type		
MP55A	M3001-3020	
MP55A	N4001-4010	Bodies and bogies by RNUR, equipment
MP55A	AB5501-5510	by CEM
MP55B	M3021-3036	
MP55B	N4011-4018	Bodies by Brissonneau et Lotz, bogies
MP55B	AB5511-5517	by Alsthom, equipment by Jeumont

Although now 35 years old, a few cars of the MP55 stock on line 11 still remain in original livery as seen here at Châtelet. On line 11 they operate in four-car formations. The numbers next to the destination blind indicate the line and train number, while the number immediately below the cab window indicates the number of the first class trailer, used to identify trains on the stabling boards. This can be seen now on most stocks, but its application, sometimes abbreviated, varies from line to line. David Rowe.

A four-car train of MP55 stock in later livery is seen at Porte des Lilas on line 11. Brian Hardy

The main difference between this stock and its predecessors lies, of course, with its bogies, but the opportunity was taken to introduce some modifications in design of the bodywork to improve the general standard of comfort offered to the travelling public. Despite being of two different batches, however, all were identical and operationally compatible.

The driving cars are 15m long, the non-driving cars and trailers 14.39m. To improve passenger flow, the width of the door openings was increased to 1.30m. The doors are operated pneumatically and can be opened by simply raising a latch as the train comes to a halt. When closing, the rate of travel slows down as the doors come together, in marked contrast to the Sprague stock, whose doors met with a hefty 'clump', and in their day no doubt accounted for many a crushed finger! Lighting and suspension were improved and, for the first time, sliding ventilators were fitted to the windows – on both sides of the car. Partly because of these, the noise level was reduced considerably. Internally, the cars were much like the articulated MA52 stock and they were painted in the same livery.

Each motor car has four 90hp axle-hung motors and JH-type cam-contactor controllers are fitted. Acceleration progresses under time control so that it is much the same whether the train is empty or full; the acceleration and deceleration rates of 1.3m/s^2 (compared with 0.7 on the Sprague stock) and 1.45m/s^2 (which can be increased to 2.5m/s^2 in emergency), together with the excellent adhesion given by rubber tyres, gives these trains very good performance, even on the severe curves and gradients of line 11.

Work on converting the trackwork on line 11 commenced in 1954 and the first train of MP55 stock entered service on 11 November 1956. Other trains followed up to October 1957. From the numbering of the stock, 17 four-car trains can be formed, leaving two driving motor cars and one non-driving motor car spare. These in fact did not enter service until required much later (3036 in February 1958, 3021 in April 1958 and 4018 in April 1961) and thus it will be appreciated that formations are not constant. This has become more evident in later years when, from 1977, a programme of renovation began, to bring the MP55 cars up to the standard of the MP73 type (q.v. below). Work included increasing the fluorescent lighting and fitting outside door indicator lights. Ventilation was also improved by fitting directional vents. The renovation of the cars was done singly and because repainting into royal blue and white livery was not necessarily done at the same time, trains could be seen in service in both liveries and in modified or unmodified form.

All cars of MP55 stock have been updated by having improved lighting fitted. The fluorescent lighting now runs the complete length of the car in this May 1992 view. Jeanne Gill

On the driving motor cars, the area surrounding the cab windows was painted black at first, presumably to give the impression of a one-piece screen that later MP stocks had. However, some have also been outshopped with white-painted cab window surrounds. The 71 vehicle fleet of MP55 stock (36 'M', 18 'N' and 17 'AB') was reduced to 64 in 1991 with the withdrawal of seven cars (3015, 3019, 3024, 3028, 4001, 4014, and 5514), with 3019, 3028 and 4014 having been out of use since 1979.

The line 11 'pneu' conversion was considered very much still an experiment, but its success prompted the RATP to begin a programme of conversion of all its lines, starting with line 1, then line 4, the two busiest Métro lines. It took a considerable period of time, however, to convert the trackwork, and then another year or so to introduce the rolling stock – the complete line's trackwork had to be converted before even one 'pneu' train could operate. On line 1, track conversion took place from 1960 and new rolling stock was introduced between 31 May 1963 and December 1964. The conversion of line 4 followed and the stock was phased in from 3 October 1966 until August 1967. The rolling stock for both lines 1 and 4 was of one type – the **MP59** – but was delivered in three batches of four groups, the last of which was not delivered until 1972/73 to supplement existing trains on those two lines for increased services. All MP59 trains were built by CIMT with ANF bogies and Jeumont equipment and were formed into six-car trains, comprising two driving motor cars (M), two non-driving motor cars (N), one composite trailer (AB) and one first class trailer (A): M – N – AB – A – N – M.

The stock was numbered as follows:

Type			
MP59A	M3037-3128	MP59C	M3159-3224
MP59A	N4019-4110	MP59C	N4141-4206
MP59A	AB5518-5563	MP59C	AB5577-5607
MP59A	A6001-6046	MP59C	A6060-6090
MP59B	M3129-3158	MP59D	M3225-3240
MP59B	N4111-4140	MP59D	N4207-4222
MP59B	AB5564-5576	MP59D	AB5608-5616
MP59B	A6047-6059	MP59D	A6091-6100

A six-car train of refurbished MP59 stock pauses at Pont de Neuilly on its way to the new line 1 terminus at La Défense. Note the new logo applied and the colourful rainbow lighting effect across the vault from recent station modernisation.
Jeanne Gill

On the line 1 extension to La Défense the railway crosses the Pont de Neuilly. A westbound train, as yet without new RATP logo, is seen on the short open-air section, looking towards Étoile. Note that the line which runs in the middle of the A14 is segregated by the high fence.
Brian Hardy

Left **A comparison in MP59 stock liveries with a refurbished car and un-refurbished car, the latter being used to move refurbished stock around Fontenay depot. Note the figure '1' on trailer A6033, then denoting first class — this was abandoned on the Métro from 1 August 1991.** Brian Hardy

Right **During refurbishment, the exteriors and interiors of MP59 stock on line 1 have been extensively altered. In this view, new lighting, vandal-resistant seating, new flooring and new sign work have been installed.** Brian Hardy

The most noticeable difference between the earlier 'pneu' trains (the MP55) on line 11 and the later ones of lines 1 and 4 (MP59) is the adoption of a wide single-span windscreen on the driving cabs of the latter trains. On these, the traction motors are rated at 140hp as against 90hp of the MP55 cars. One of the additional trains built in 1973 (3235-4217-6069-5613-4218-3236) was equipped with thyristor 'chopper' control, operating in service on line 1 until 1979, then on line 4. It was sub-classified MP59DK and was converted to MP59D standard in 1985.

The original six-car formations of the MP59 stock comprised one trailer car ('A') and one-third of the adjacent trailer ('AB') with first class accommodation. During 1981–83, all the composite ('AB') cars on line 1 and 4 were converted to second class, giving one car out of six available for first class passengers, (compared to one out of five cars on most other lines). From 1 March 1982, first class travel on all lines was restricted to between the hours of 09.00 and 17.00 daily. Previously it had applied from 08.00 and then throughout each day until the end of service. Insofar as the MP59 'AB' trailers were concerned, all that needed to be done was to alter the interior and exterior '1' to '2' on the old livery cars and to remove the appropriate section of yellow band from the newer liveried cars. When first class on the Métro was abolished altogether from 1 August 1991 a similar operation followed on the relevant cars.

The original fleet of 607 MP59 cars (204 'M', 204 'N', 99 'AB' and 100 'A') has been reduced by three over the years, due to various mishaps. N4077 was withdrawn in 1977, N4069 in 1982 and M3073 in 1986.

For reasons that will become apparent in the next rolling stock section (MF67), the RATP decided to abandon its plan to convert all Métro lines to 'pneu' operation, but a change of heart was made for line 6, which has much more open-air running (mostly on viaduct) than any other Métro line. This gave much noise and vibration with the old Sprague stock and this line was therefore an ideal candidate for rubber-tyred trains. Track conversion commenced in 1972 and new rolling stock of type **MP73** was built by CIMT with ANF bogies and Jeumont equipment. Surprisingly, for a rubber-tyred line, the rolling stock was introduced within the space of just one month – from July 1974 (the period of the year with the lowest peak traffic) with extra trains added in time for maximum winter service, which starts in October. Trains were formed into five cars: M – B – A – N – M. The bodywork design was based on the already successful MF67 stock (q.v. below), which by then had become the accepted design for new stock until the advent of the MF77 type. The cars were numbered as follows:

M3501 - 3602   N4501 - 4550   A6501 - 6550   B7001 - 7050

Left **A five-car train of MP73 stock on line 6 approaches Bir-Hakeim, having crossed the Passy viaduct. The unique Passy station can be seen in the background.** Brian Hardy

Right **Interior of an MP73 'B' trailer car, showing the main passenger seats in facing pairs, and pairs of tip-up seats by the door openings.** Brian Hardy

The Paris Métro is renowned for its sharp curves, when following the line of streets. Certain open sections of line 6 are no exception as seen at Corvisart with a train for Nation arriving on 8 May 1992. Brian Hardy

Some trains of MP73 stock have been allocated to line 11 since January 1976, to supplement the MP55 trains and providing an increased service on that line. The MP73 sets on line 11 operate in four-car formation like their MP55 counterparts, with the spare (fifth) cars being stored. A small number of MP73 train sets also operated on line 4 between 1975 and 1979.

The MP73 stock can thus mostly be found on line 6 and as this line contains several open-air sections, amounting to almost half the line's length, special features were incorporated in these trains. This includes weatherproof ventilation, windscreen wipers, grooved tyres, snowproof resistance grids and chassis parts in Corten rustproof alloy instead of steel. This was the first new stock for the Paris Métro to be delivered in the new royal blue and white livery, with a dark blue stripe at waist level, and first class indicated by a yellow band at roof line. Outside door indicator lights are fitted to these trains, after an experiment with a train of MP59 stock on line 4 (3231-4213-6001-(7004)-4214-3232), which incorporates an MP73 trailer.

A small number of trains of MP73 stock are allocated to line 11 and operate in four-car formations. A train is seen at Châtelet, the in-town terminus of the line. Brian Hardy

It is interesting to note that M3599/3600 served as prototypes for the Marseille Métro, and M3602 for the Lyon Métro. In addition, cars A6550 and N4550, both having experimental suspension, first entered service on line 1 with the MP59 stock and were painted in the old livery of that stock, while the rest of the MP73 type was in the royal blue and white livery. Both cars were repainted into standard colours when they went into service on line 6 in 1976.

The MP73 stock fleet today comprises 250 cars of four types, as follows, and excludes two cars which have been withdrawn – A6504 in 1977 and A6550 (1991).

MP73A		MP73P1	MP73P2	MP86 Prototype
M3501–3598	A6501–6503	M3602	N4550	M3599–3600
M3601	A6505–6549		B7050	
N4501–4549	B7001–7049			

The MP59 stock has, since new, been confined to a tunnel working environment on lines 1 and 4, but the new extension of line 1 westwards to La Défense entailed adapting the line 1 MP59 fleet for the small section of open-air running between Pont de Neuilly and Esplanade de la Défense and providing some extra trains for service. The latter was achieved by reinstating the train used at Porte des Lilas for instruction as well as some spare MP73 trailer ('B') cars. This allowed a float of trains to be provided for the MP59 trains on line 1 to be refurbished which would also, at the end of the programme, provide the extra trains needed to operate the extended line. Following a prototype conversion with motor car M3125 in 1989, 52 trains were refurbished during the 1990–92 period, 22 by 'Cannes La Bocca Industries' and 23 by 'Ateliers de Constructions du Centre' of Clermont Ferrand (all of which had to be transported from and back to Fontenay depot by road), plus seven at the RATP's Fontenay depot. All 52 trains, however, are identical after refurbishment. The interiors have been totally renovated with new materials to combat graffiti and have vandal-proof seats. Additional fluorescent lighting has been installed and the roof-mounted ventilation has been weather-proofed. Cosmetic alterations have been made to the driving cab fronts to give a 'one-piece' appearance, the all-black front picked out by an all-round beading line. The car bodies themselves have been repainted in white, with the passenger doors in blue.

The MF67 Stock

While the success of the rubber-tyred stock was undoubted, it took approximately three years to convert the trackwork and generally about another year to phase in the rolling stock, and at that rate it would have been impossible to have completed the modernisation of the Métro before the end of this century. Between 1951 and 1964 there were, too, considerable advances in the design of conventional rapid transit trains in other countries, and in 1964 the RATP began to study the development of modern rolling stock which would provide the same acceleration and braking characteristics, as well as the quiet and comfortable ride, as the 'pneu' trains. The result was the **MF67** stock, the first train of which went into service on line 3 on 21 December 1967.

Externally, the MF67 stock differed from the 'pneu' trains only in the restyled front end and driver's cab, and in its pull-down opening saloon windows instead of sliding vents. The trains are much quieter than the Classic stock; some have rubber sandwich wheels, a ring of rubber blocks being pressed between the steel tyres and the rims of the wheels. Rubber springing in the bogies and sound insulation of the bodies also contribute to the reduction of noise.

The first recipient of MF67 stock was line 3. At the western terminus of Pont de Lavallois a train in original livery arrives, while a train in the newer livery awaits departure. Some Métro terminal stations have a platform track which also has a pit for inspection purposes, as trains are stabled overnight on the line and not in depots. Brian Hardy

The MF67 cars have all axles driven and originally trains were formed of motor cars only, to give a performance approximate to that of the 'pneu' stock. Half the cars have monomotor bogies with a 194hp motor and half have two-motor bogies with two 99hp motors. Control is by servo-motor-operated cam-contactors with electronic control of the servo-motors to give smooth acceleration. Service braking is rheostatic down to low speeds with air taking over thereafter. In practice, the provision of all-motor-car trains proved to be over-generous and trailers were subsequently introduced in 1974. Normal train formation is now three motor cars and two trailers in a five-car set. Modifications introduced on successive batches of motor cars include regenerative braking, mechanical ventilation, disc brakes and air suspension. Internally, the MF67 stock has generous lighting by fluorescent tubes and comfortable leatherette seating. Some of the prototypes, however, have a different cosmetic finish. Loudspeakers allow the driver to address the passengers and the MF67E stock on line 2 has been modified so that there is two-way communication between the driver and passengers should an emergency handle be operated, a feature first adopted on the MF77 trains. Door indicator lights are fitted to the car exteriors, so that staff can easily identify faulty doors.

Whilst in general terms the MF67 type is grouped into six sub classes, (generally designated MF67A to MF67F) when analysed in depth there are in fact 15 different types, each having slight differences, generally in equipment, but sometimes in cosmetic finishes. For example, one train was delivered in unpainted aluminium/stainless steel.

Following the entry into service of the first (prototype) train (type 'W1') on line 3 in December 1967, production started of the 'A' series, entering service on line 3 from August 1968, formed into five-car sets: M – N – NA – N – M. The order also comprised the unpainted/stainless steel train (type 'W2') and six single cars of types 'B1' and 'B2'. The 'A' series comprised two types – the 'A1' with monomotor bogies and the 'A2' with bi-motor bogies. The last of this series went into service on line 3 in January 1970, making a total of 42 five-car trains, including the prototypes and the experimental cars.

The next line to receive MF67 stock was line 7 from June 1971. Prior to this, a new series of MF67 stock commenced delivery – the 'C1' – from early-1971, first entering service on line 3 from April. This allowed the release of the 'A2' type from line 3 to line 7 and from December 1971 a further new batch of type 'C2' entered service directly on line 7, the last to do so being in January 1974. This segregated the stocks so that the trains with monomotor bogies were all on line 3 and those with bi-motors were on line 7. All three types 'A', 'B' and 'C' and their variations were built by CIMT and Brissonneau et Lotz.

Six three-car trains of MF67C-D stock are allocated to line 3bis for the short trip between Porte des Lilas (seen here) and Gambetta, which takes a little over three minutes. Four trains are required for the peak service. Brian Hardy

Included in the prototype cars and trains were two trailers, one of which was finished in unpainted aluminium/stainless steel. These two trailers entered service in late 1969 and early 1970 to evaluate the performance of trains that were not formed of all motor cars, being transferred to line 7 in November 1971.

The dilution of train sets with trailers was successful and it allowed the RATP to reduce both capital and operating costs. The next order for MF67 stock therefore comprised all trailers – both driving and non-driving – built jointly by Alsthom and SFB from mid-1974 to early 1976, the first examples entering service on line 3 in September 1974 (trailers) and on line 9 (driving trailers). These trailers (156 driving trailers coded 'S', 145 second class trailers coded 'B' and 62 first class trailers coded 'A') were known as MF67 type 'D'.

A carefully prepared plan involving the reformation of the all-motor sets on lines 3 and 7 was implemented. On line 3, the two 'N' cars were removed and replaced by 'B' trailers, giving a formation of M – B – NA – B – M. On line 7, one 'N' and one 'NA' was removed and replaced by a new 'B' and 'A' respectively, giving a formation of M – B – A – N – M. The new driving trailers ('S') were formed with displaced 'N' and 'NA' cars, forming trains thus: S – N – NA – N – S. These went into service on lines 9 and 13, with a small allocation to line 10 to supplement the articulated stock then being transferred from line 13. To complete this plan, four non driving motors (N11131-11134) were converted to first class accommodation, becoming NA12129-12132 in 1974. It is interesting to note that the MF67D stock had to be delivered in the old pale blue livery (first class cars cream) to match the older cars of MF67 stock that they were being formed with, even though previous new stock (the MP73 for line 6) had been delivered in the new royal blue and white livery.

A further two batches of MF67 stock were yet to be built, but these were not generally to be mixed with the A-D type. The next batch was the MF67 type 'E' and these five car trains in the new livery from new were built by CIMT and entered service on line 8 from 14 July 1975, with some going to line 13. The delivery of this stock to line 8 allowed some of the grey Sprague stock to be transferred to line 2 (and later, lines 9 and 12), then seeing the end of two-motor Sprague stock on line 2 on 22 March 1976.

The final batch of MF67 stock was the type 'F', built by BL. These trains, also five cars in length, had interior fans fitted for improved ventilation and were instantly recognisable from the outside, by having a smoother finish to the roof line. They first entered service on line 13 from October 1976, displacing the MF67E type on that line, to join their sister cars on line 8.

With the advent of the MF77 stock, which first went to line 13, the displaced MF67F trains were transferred to line 7, which allowed the diluted M – B – A – N – M formations of the A–D type to be transferred to lines 9 and 12. In fact both these lines operated formations of M – B – A – N – M and S – N – NA – N – S. Some of the latter driving trailer sets also went to line 5 from April 1978, and to line 2 from February 1979.

Deliveries of the MF77 stock then went to lines 7 (from September 1979) and 8 (from July 1980), which released the MF67F from line 7 to go to line 5, and the MF67E from line 8 to line 2. The earlier A-D types on line 2 went to line 12, finishing off the Sprague stock on that line in December 1980, followed by line 2 in June 1981. Enough MF67F trains were available from line 7 to replace the Sprague stock on line 7bis from July 1980, which operated in full-length five-car formations, while from mid-1981 a sufficient number of MF67E trains were available to replace the Sprague stock on line 3bis, but in three-car formations, the other two cars of the set being stored. To give a section of first class accommodation on these three-car sets, a small portion of the middle trailer was converted as such and were temporarily classified as 'Ba'. This arrangement on the two branch lines was short-lived and a more permanent stock situation was established. From February 1982, the five-car trains of MF67F stock on line 7bis were transferred back to line 7 (and subsequently to line 5), being replaced by four-car sets of MF67E from line 3bis, the first class trailer in the formation being brought back out of store. On line 3bis, three-car trains of MF67A-D type were transferred in from line 9, in the same formation of M-Ba-M.

The open-air stabling of the MF67F trains on line 5 at Bobigny from 1985 soon highlighted corrosion problems in the door pocket areas on these trains and thus between 1987 and 1989 all were modified at Vaugirard depot with enclosed windows at the door slide-back positions, giving a 'double-glazed' appearance. In each seated area of the saloon, a narrow section for window opening was provided.

Recent changes to the MF67 stock have been very few. However, some conversions of car types has taken place. On line 9, MF67C2A cars N11005 and NA12003 have been de-motored to become trailers B14159 and A13073 respectively, while A13069, A13067 and A13061 have become (respectively) B14156–B14158. In addition, N11226 has been withdrawn.

The MF67 stock can now be found in service on eight Métro lines, in the following formations:

	Type	Formation
Line 2	MF67E	M — B — A — N — M
Line 3	MF67A-D	M — B — NA — B — M*
Line 3bis	MF67A-D	M — Ba — M
Line 5	MF67F	M — N — A — B — M‡
Line 7bis	MF67E	M — N — A — M
Line 9	MF67A-D	S — N — NA — N — S
	MF67A-D	M — N — A — B — M
Line 10	MF67A-D	S — N — NA — N — S§
Line 12	MF67A-D	S — N — NA — N — S

*2 trains are M – N – NA – N – M
‡1 train M – N – NA – N – S, 1 train S – N – NA – N – S (both MF67A–D)
§1 train S – N – N – N – S
It should be noted that any reference to first class cars (A/NA/Ba) is now superfluous, although the legends continue to be used.

MF67 STOCK SUMMARY

Stock Type	M	N	NA	A	B	S	Total
MF67 W1	2	2	1	–	1	–	6
MF67 W2	2	2	1	–	1	–	6
MF67 A1	36	40	20	–	–	–	96
MF67 A2	39	39	20	–	–	–	98
MF67 B1	4	–	–	–	–	–	4
MF67 B2	1	1	–	–	–	–	2
MF67 C1	44	40	26	–	–	–	110
MF67 C1A	2	2	1	–	–	–	5
MF67 C2	91	91	46	–	–	–	228
MF67 C2A	2	1	–	1	1	–	5
MF67 CS	2	1	1	–	–	–	4
MF67 CX	–	7	9	–	–	–	16
MF67 D	–	–	–	59	148	156	363
MF67 E	114	56	–	56	56	–	282
MF67 F	104	51	–	51	51	–	257
Total:	443	333	125	167	258	156	1482

Since the last edition of this handbook three surplus first class trailers of MF67D stock have been converted to second class trailers. In November 1991 A13061, seen here in Fontenay depot, was awaiting conversion to become B14158.
Brian Hardy

The unpainted aluminium prototype train of MF67W2 stock is now in use for instruction purposes. It is seen when in service on line 9 at Miromesnil.
Brian Hardy

The sixth unpainted aluminium MF67W2 car, B14002, has been painted for some time, running in service on line 3 since 1979. In June 1991 however, it assumed duties as part of a train used for instructional purposes. Brian Hardy

In service on line 3 as a complete five-car train is the prototype MF67C1A, recognisable from the outside by its smooth roof line. The train is seen at Opéra, a station which was built using the cut-and-cover method, as demonstrated by the girder roof. Brian Hardy

The services on lines 2 and 7bis are operated by trains of MF67E stock. Seen leaving La Chapelle a train heads for Porte Dauphine on 25 December 1991. The Métro operates every day of the year from 05.30 to 01.15, including Christmas Day, when line 2 was as busy as always! The Sacre Couer can be seen overlooking the Métro. Jeanne Gill

The last batch of MF67 stock was type F of 1976-78 vintage, and all is now at work on line 5. It differs visibly from other MF67 trains by having a flush roof line containing vents. At Quai de la Rapée a Bobigny bound train is seen (right) with a southbound train to Place d'Italie arriving. The train on the right clearly shows the double-glazing that was necessary on this stock to enclose the door slide-back areas to prevent corrosion with the open-air stabling sidings at Bobigny. Brian Hardy

The numbers and 15 variations of the MF67 Stock can be summarised as follows:

Type	Numbers	New	Details
MF67W1	M10001-10002	1967	Built by CIMT, Düwag monomotor bogies,
	N11001-11002	1967	CEM and Siemens equipment. B14001 has
	NA12001	1967	MF77 type interior.
	B14001	1970	
MF67W2	M10003-10004	1968	Built by Brissonneau et Lotz, ANF bimotor
	N11003-11004	1968	bogies, Alsthom equipment. Stainless steel/
	NA12002	1968	unpainted body by Carel-Fouché, saving
	B14002	1969	700kg weight per car, but more expensive to
			produce and therefore not pursued. B14002
			now repainted into the new blue livery.
MF67A1	M10011-10019	1968	Built by CIMT, Düwag monomotor bogies,
	M10021-10023	1968	CEM equipment. Rheostatic/disc braking.
	M10026-10027	1968	
	M10029-10050	1968	
	N11011-11050	1968	
	NA12011-12030	1968	
MF67A2	M10051-10053	1969	Built by Brissonneau et Lotz, ANF bimotor
	M10055-10090	1969	bogies, Alsthom equipment. Coventional
	N11051-11053	1969	brake blocks, rheostatic braking.
	N11055-11090	1969	
MF67B1	M10020	1969	Built by Brissonneau et Lotz, CEM equip-
	M10024-10025	1969	ment. Experimental monomotor bogies by
	M10028	1969	MTE (10020), Alsthom (10024), ANF (10025)
			and CAFL (10028).
MF67B2	M10054	1969	Built by Brissonneau et Lotz, Alsthom equip-
	N11054	1969	ment, ANF bimotor bogies with air suspen-
			sion.
MF67C1	M10091-10134	1971	CIMT bodies and monomotor bogies, CEM
	N11091-11134	1971	equipment. Rheostatic/disc braking.
	NA12051-12072	1971	Note: N11131-11134 now NA12129-12132
		1971	
MF67C1A	M10007-10008	1973	CIMT aluminium bodies, Düwag monomotor
	N11007-11008	1973	bogies, CEM/Jeumont equipment, pneumatic
	NA12004	1973	suspension, interior fans for mechanical ven-
			tilation.
MF67C2	M10135-10224	1971	Built by Brissonneau et Lotz, ANF bimotor
	M10227	1971	bogies, Alsthom equipment, conventional
	N11135-11224	1971	brake blocks, rheostatic braking.
	N11227	1971	
	NA12073-12118	1971	
MF67C2A	M10005-10006	1974	Built by Brissonneau et Lotz, ANF bimotor
	N11005-11006	1974	bogies, Alsthom equipment, pneumatic sus-
	NA12003	1974	pension and mechanical ventilation.
			Note: N11005 now B14159 and NA12003
			now A13073

MF67CS	M10225-10226	1975	Built by Brissonneau et Lotz, MTE bogies
	N11225-11226	1975	with pneumatic suspension, Alsthom equip-
	NA12119	1975	ment, regenerative normal service braking
			and electro magnetic braking.
MF67CX	N11228-11234	1974	As type C2, but N11228 and 11234 fitted
	NA12120-12128	1974	with plug doors, as similarly adopted on
			MF77 stock trains.
MF67D	S9011-9126	1974	Built by Alsthom.
	A13011-13052	1974	
	B14011-14114	1974	
MF67D	S9127-9166	1974	Built by CIMT. Note: A13061, 13067, 13069,
	A13053-13072	1974	now B14158, 14157, 14156 respectively.
	B14115-14155	1974	
MF67E	M10301-10414	1975	Built by CIMT, ANF bimotor bogies,
	N11301-11356	1975	Alsthom equipment, regenerative braking.
	A13301-13356	1975	First of MF67 type to be delivered in new
	B14301-14356	1975	royal blue/white livery. Bogies on N11332
			and M10370 by Creusot Loire. B14311 with
			concealed lighting, fans and MI79 type grab
			stands/perches.
MF67F	M10501-10604	1976	Built by Brissonneau et Lotz, ANF mono-
	N11501-11551	1976	motor bogies with pneumatic suspension,
	A13501-13551	1976	TCO equipment, disc/regenerative braking.
	B14501-14551	1976	Interior fans for mechanical ventilation,
			giving a smoother finish to the exterior
			roof line.

Left **An interior view of MF67E stock, showing its similarity to its previous sister cars and also the MP73 stock of the same era.** Brian Hardy

Right **The last batch of MF67 stock was fitted with interior fans, which can be seen along the centre of the car roof between the fluorescent lighting. The darker seating seen here perhaps makes it look a little austere?** Brian Hardy

The trains of MF77 stock were the first to have sloping body sides to give maximum width at waist level. Seen on line 8, a train is stabled adjacent to Créteil-l'Echat. David Rowe

The MF77 Stock

The extension of the Métro into the suburbs of Paris and the greater distance between stations on these extensions (800 to 1,000m as against about 500m in the City area) highlighted some of the weak points of existing designs and in 1972 the RATP instituted studies for the design of rolling stock which would be faster and more comfortable than existing trains, and more suited to suburban work. Experiments with various features, such as plug doors, internal decor etc, were made on various cars of MF67 stock and research was undertaken by industrial designers, acting in collaboration with both engineers and marketing specialists, and backed by surveys made among the travelling public to find out what they wanted in the new trains. A mock-up coach was built and exhibited at the 75th anniversary of the Métro at Porte Maillot station in 1975 which was in green and brown livery. The result of all this was the **MF77** stock, the first train of which entered service on line 13 in September 1978. The trains are formed into five-car sets (M – B – NA – B – M) and can now be found operating the complete services on lines 7, 8 and 13.

When the new trains appeared they showed an advance in design not only over existing Métro stock, but also over trains running on rapid transit systems elsewhere. The sides of the cars are not straight, unlike all previous Métro stock, but curve outwards to give the maximum width at waist level consistent with the constraints of the loading gauge. This, together with the use of plug-type doors instead of ones sliding back into recesses, has given a total increase in width of 140mm at the shoulder level of seated passengers. The unusual (for Paris Métro) shape of the cars is set off by a striking livery of off-white, relieved only by dark blue panels round the windscreens of the driving motor cars. First class accommodation was indicated by a yellow band at cantrail level. The cars are also slightly longer (15.110m on motor cars and 15.120m on trailers and non-driving motor

The MF77 trains were built to the maximum possible loading gauge. The wide double passenger doors open outwards and slide back against the body exterior. The train seen here at Miromesnil is going to Saint-Denis (white-on-blue destination). Trains to the other northern line 13 branch (which may eventually become part of the new Météor line) at Asnières Gennevilliers would be shown in black-on-yellow. Brian Hardy

An interior view of MF77 stock looking towards the driving cab and showing that the fluorescent lighting is concealed behind ceiling grilles. Note that the seating on this stock is arranged in individual pairs. Jeanne Gill

cars) and in fact at some of the shorter stations, the head of the train is actually in the tunnel during stops. The new cars have only three pairs of doors per side as against four in previous stocks, but the door openings are much wider, at 1.575m instead of 1.30m, thus allowing a rapid flow of passengers. Push-button door control, comprising a button concealed in a shell grip, allows passengers to open individual pairs of doors once the train has stopped at a station, rather than by lifting a latch as hitherto.

Internally, the MF77 trains are distinguished by a harmony of muted tones, in contrast to the striking colour schemes favoured for other contemporary stock elsewhere. The seat colour is dark blue, walls are light blue and the doors, grab rails etc., are finished in stainless steel. The floors are covered with rubber matting. The space between the seats has been increased from 48cm to 54cm, to give improved comfort to seated passengers. All the materials used in the interior furnishings are, or have been treated to be, fire resistant. Lighting is by fluorescent tubes but, to reduce glare, is placed behind grilles which run the length of the ceiling and incorporate fans for ventilation. Seating is provided by individual pairs of seats instead of pairs of benches, and those at the non-driving ends of the cars are arranged in groups of three to face each other, giving the effect of a small saloon. The former tip-up perches have been replaced by proper folding seats, just as comfortable as the main seating. Heating and ventilation is thermostatically controlled. In addition to the windows in the communicating doors between the cars, windows are also provided either side of these at the trailing ends. This helps to create an atmosphere of spaciousness and a feeling of security which, with the high standard of design, gives a pleasant and relaxing effect overall.

The car body is made of light alloy sections, giving a saving of two tonnes in weight over a comparable train of steel construction. The driving cabs of the trains were designed after considerable ergonomic study and are laid out in such a way as to afford maximum convenience and comfort to the drivers. As on stock since the MP55 type, a speedometer and tachograph are fitted and three groups of colour light signals convey information about the running of the train and the functioning or non-functioning, of the equipment. As on all modern stock, a high-frequency telephone link keeps the drivers in touch with the PCC, but an innovation on the MF77 stock is a two-way link bewteen the driver and passengers, which comes into action when the emergency alarm signal has been actuated, in addition to the normal public address equipment.

The MF77 trains were built by SFB and Alsthom, the main order comprising 187 five-car trains, between 1978 and 1982. A further order for ten trains was built by Alsthom in 1986, to provide the stock required for the extensions to line 7. The MF77 trains are fitted with MTE-type bogies of the type already in use on the MF67F trains. Equipment is provided by TCO. There are six motor bogies on each five-car train and each motor bogie has a 266kW motor installed lengthwise between the two axles, in the centre of the bogie frame. On motor cars there is regenerative braking, plus air brakes, while on trailers braking is by compressed air alone.

Traction and braking control is performed by thyristor-equipped current choppers. The choppers do away with rheostats, which had hitherto been used to start the motors. They ensure far greater operating versatility and also cut down consumption while enabling power to be recovered on braking furnished by the motors operating as generators, which is fed back to the power line. Thus, the energy saving on a line equipped with modern cars can reach 40% compared with conventional trains with rheostatic starting and devoid of regenerative braking. In this way, the energy which was unnecessarily dissipated as heat is now recovered, the temperature in the Métro is reduced and comfort is enhanced.

The first train of MF77 stock was made available to the press at the SFB factory in Valenciennes on 25 October 1977, and in December it was exhibited to the public at Châtelet-les-Halles station on the RER. The first train to be delivered to Vaugirard depot arrived on 23 June 1978, and underwent exhaustive testing. Deliveries allowed the first train to enter service on line 13 in September 1978 and the following year line 7 was the next recipient of the MF77 stock, although it was not until 1985 that the last of the MF67F type was transferred away from line 7 to line 5. Line 13 had all MF77 trains by the end of 1979. In 1980 line 8 began to receive MF77 stock, replacing the MF67E type.

The last train of the main order of MF77 stock entered service on 2 February 1983 and subsequently allowed, through cascades of other stock, the last of the Sprague stock to be withdrawn.

The additional ten trains of MF77 stock for the line 7 extensions were delivered between September 1985 and July 1986, all entering service (on line 13, with other MF77 trains transferred to line 7) during 1986.

Built by SFB:

M30001-30074	B32001-32074	NA31001-31037
M30119-30158	B32119-32158	NA31060-31079
M30219-30252	B32219-32252	NA31110-31126
M30295-30328	B32295-32328	NA31148-31164
M30365-30370	B32365-32370	NA31183-31185

Built by Alsthom:

M30075-30118	B32075-32118	NA31038-31059
M30159-30218	B32159-32218	NA31080-31109
M30253-30294	B32253-32294	NA31127-31147
M30329-30364	B32329-32364	NA31165-31182
M30371-30374	B32371-32374	NA31186-31187
M30375-30394*	B32375-32394*	NA31188-31197*

Note * 1985–86 batch

M30154 and B32154 scrapped April 1984.

For the future a large order of new 'pneu' stock has been placed with GEC Alsthom of type **MP89**. The new trains will be for line 1 (which will allow the refurbished trains of MP59 stock to be transferred to line 4, replacing their unrefurbished counterparts), line 11 (replacing the very first 'pneu' stock – the MP55 type) and for the new Météor line (q.v. Chapter 7).

Six car trains of MP89 stock will operate on line 1 in the formation S–N–N–N–N–S and five cars on line 11 (S–N–N–N–S). The driving trailers will be 15.38m long and the intermediate non-driving motors 14.88m long. Each six-car train will have a capacity for 694 passengers (136 seated) and each five-car train 576 (112 seated), all based on a maximum loading of 4 passengers/m^2. There will be complete intercirculation between all cars in each train set, and the articulated gangways are being built by Faiveley.

Initially six-car trains will operate the new Météor line, but as it will be a completely no-person-operated line, there is no need for the provision of a driving cab. Instead, at the outer ends of each train, there will be a trailer (identical in appearance to the conventional MP89 driving trailers on lines 1 and 11) but with an emergency driving desk only. Train formations will thus be Sp–N–N–N–N–Sp. The additional space created by the absence of a cab in the 'Sp' cars will mean the capacity of a six-car train will be 708 passengers (144 seated).

A full-size mock up of an MP89 car was taken to Stockholm for exhibition at the 49th UITP congress between 3–6 June 1992.

Delivery of two prototype MP89 trains was made in December 1992. The present order comprises 665 cars, as follows:

52 x 6 cars for line 1	S–N–N–N–N–S
19 x 5 cars for line 11	S–N–N–N–S
43 x 6 cars for Météor	Sp–N–N–N–N– Sp

When the Météor line becomes fully operational, eight-car trains are envisaged, which will require additional 'B' and 'N' type vehicles, giving the train formation Sp–N–N–B–N–N–N– Sp.

The train of the future is the MP89 stock for lines 1 and 11 and the new Météor line, the latter having no conventional driving controls. This view of the mock-up shows how this stock might look, first being unveiled in 1992. RATP

Below An interior of the MP89 mock-up looking towards the front of the train. It is presumed that on the Météor trains passengers will have a view looking forwards as the trains will be fully automatic with only an emergency driving desk provided. RATP

Although the 'BOA' train operates in service on line 5 during the midday off peak on Mondays to Fridays, it also worked a shuttle service on line 12 in November 1991 from Porte de Versailles into Vaugirard depot during an open-day. Julian Pepinster

The prototype BOA has three experimental connections between the four body sections. The left view shows the example by Faiveley and also demonstrates how trains are moved in depot yards where there are no current rails. A pole, which has an attachment to the train is placed on an overhead wire as seen here. The centre view, shows the ANF connection while the picture on the right shows that by Alsthom, which also contains windows and seats. This train is fitted with steerable axles instead of conventional bogies. Brian Hardy

The first three-car train of MF88 stock was delivered by road on 18/21/22 December 1992. It is seen at Porte des Lilas on 14 January 1993 while undergoing tests on the former shuttle line, which closed in 1939. Brian Hardy

The Future

The RATP have been actively engaged in planning for future Métro rolling stock since 1980, of the steel-wheel-on-steel-rail type. The results of studies and tests is the 'BOA', a fully articulated train using single axles instead of bogies, thus providing the train with steered axles without the extra weight and complication of a steerable bogie. The first prototype train was designed and built by the RATP themselves in Vaugirard depot and consisted of three 10m articulated cars with monomotor axles. Apart from the articulation and the inter-connection between axles, all parts used were already on other stocks, being well-tried and tested. For instance, the underfloor equipment is as used on MP73 stock, and the car bodies are most definitely MF77.

Tests recommenced in February 1985, the new innovation being a great success. With the reduction in the weight of the train, it consumes less current and stress on curves is much reduced. It was also tested on the very sharp non-passenger loop at Porte Dauphine on line 2 without problems. Early in 1986 the system was adapted to have steerable axles at the front of the train instead of bogies, whereby the leading axle 'reads' the curvature of the track and then guides the second axle. The leading axle is non-load-bearing and has smaller wheels than on all other axles.

Following on from these tests, the next stage was to develop a train which would ultimately carry passengers and the original 'BOA' was returned to Vaugirard workshops to enable a four-bodied train to be constructed. This enabled three different types of body articulation to be tested, one each by Faiveley, ANF and Alsthom. That by Faiveley comprises an elastic assembly made of rubber with distortable joints, the ANF example having a distortable assembly made of rigid and flexible frames and the Alsthom (RATP Patent) articulated gangway has a rigid assembly articulated at both ends between car bodies. The last two articulations each contain seats and the Alsthom gangway incorporates side windows. All seats are of the tip-up type. The four-body section thus allows complete intercirculation by passengers.

The driving motor cars are 12.19m long and the non-driving motors 10.98m long, making the four-body train 46.34m long overall. Tests resumed in 1987 and subsequently it was decided that it would operate on trial on line 5. Empty running commenced on 12 November 1990 and passengers were carried for the first time on 31 December 1990. Because the train is much shorter than normal-length trains on line 5 and because it is not equipped for automatic driving, its operation is confined to off-peak periods Mondays to Fridays with two morning and one afternoon round trips being worked from Bobigny to Place d'Italie on an 'as required' basis.

Also being tested is the use of asynchronous motors on this train, following trials on MF77 driving motor car M30125 and MF67 cars M10024 and M10025.

The BOA train which bears the numbers M30411–N11552–N11553– M30412 has thus been the testbed and prototype for the future **MF88** stock for line 7bis, which will ultimately allow through consequential inter-line stock transfers, the withdrawal of the articulated MA52 stock – the oldest type now in service on the Métro. The first three-car train of the production MF88 stock was delivered to Bobigny depot by road in late-December 1992. A total of nine trains are being built by ANF with inter-car connections built by Faiveley. These nine trains will be used in service, but will be modified as necessary as time progresses to provide the information and experience required to enable the replacement of the MF67 stock at the turn of the century. Finished in jade-green, white and black, entry into service is anticipated from the summer of 1993.

CHAPTER FIVE
MÉTRO OPERATIONS

Signalling

As far as can be ascertained, line 1 was opened for traffic without the protection of signals of any kind. As there were only ten trains operating on a ten or twelve minute headway, a time interval system apparently sufficed. However, on 20 September 1900, a new timetable doubled the service and it seems that this coincided with the adoption of a full system of signalling.

The first system to be adopted was the Hall block system, a mechanical one in which the signals were set by the passage of trains. The leading wheel of the first coach depressed a treadle at the side of the track and this in turn activated the signal arm, causing a disc to move and change the signal to caution (green). It also changed the last signal but one to clear (white). A green signal could be passed at reduced speed. Not surprisingly, this was open to abuse and on 19 October 1900 there was a rear-end collision between Champs-Élysées and Concorde, when a train set back and was run into by the following one, which was running under clear signals. Fortunately, there was no serious injury to passengers or crew. The green signal indications were then replaced by red and it was forbidden to pass a red signal except on written order, and then at only 10 km/hour. When line 2 (Nord) was opened, the system was modified further and the signals remained normally at red, clearing to white only immediately in front of a train and so avoiding any confusion with street lamps on the overhead section. The elevated part of line 2 Sud used semaphore signals similar to those of the main line railways. With careful maintenance, the Hall system worked quite well, but the trackside treadles were very easily put out of alignment and its use was not further extended after the opening of line 3.

Its successor was known as the Métro automatic block system. In this, a bar about five metres long was placed parallel to the running rails, on the opposite side of the track to the third rail. When energised by contact with the collector shoe of a passing train, the bar transmitted an electrical impulse, changing the signal to clear or danger as required. The system was installed on lines 4 to 8 as they were opened and between 1914 and 1918 replaced the Hall signalling on lines 1, 2 (Nord and Sud) and 3.

The Nord-Sud company, ever independent, made use of an entirely different system based on track circuits and relays. The entry of a train into a section caused a short circuit and cut off current from the relays, putting the signal at danger behind the train. It remained so until the train had cleared the next section ahead. At stations, three aspect signals were used, a green distant allowing entry to the station at reduced speed as soon as the preceding train had left. At the exits from stations there were two red indications and one white, one red being extinguished to allow departure when the train ahead had cleared the first section. The three aspect signals were ultimately introduced on the CMP, but the track circuits were given up in 1932, two years after the Nord-Sud was taken over.

From 1921, the CMP had in fact adopted a very similar system, but using alternating current for the track circuits rather than direct current. Unlike both the previous Métro block and the Nord-Sud systems, signals were normally clear, and changed to danger only with the passage of a train. The system was first used on line 9, and all other lines had been converted to it by 1942. Relays with proving contacts were used from 1928 onwards to provide added safety.

After 1945, it was necessary to renew the signalling and the opportunity was taken to adopt the internationally-accepted colours of red, yellow and green. Green distant signals were replaced by yellow aspects in March 1955 and in turn, green replaced white as the 'line clear' indication in April of the same year. More recently, the adoption of continuously-welded rail had made it necessary to adopt high-frequency current, at different frequencies in adjacent sections, for the signalling.

Today, the normal signal on the Métro is the two aspect colour light block (or 'spacing') signal, giving a green or red aspect according to the track circuit. At the entry to busier stations, three aspect signals are often found, in which a yellow indication allows entry to the station at reduced speed when the preceding train has just cleared it. In certain places, this signal is supplemented by a preceding intermediate signal, whose function is to anticipate the clearing of the station and which, when clear, allows a train to approach a station when the rear of the preceding train is half-way along the platform. These signals are generally protected by an outer two aspect signal, which remains at red when the others have cleared. On curves and other areas of reduced visibility, repeater signals are provided, giving yellow and green aspects only and are worked in conjunction with the block signal ahead. In all cases, a train is protected in the rear by two red signals, except at entry to stations as mentioned above.

Train stops have not been used at any time on the Métro, but since the days of the Hall signalling system, any train which has passed a signal at danger has set off a bell and a visual indication in the next station. These can be cut off only by the station staff and such incidents have to be reported in writing.

There were few shunting signals in the early days, but a system developed as terminal layouts grew more complex, quite independent of the running signals. Following a collision at Porte des Lilas in 1949, when a driver confused a shunting signal with a block signal and passed the latter at red, block signals have generally been removed from these areas, leaving only the shunting signals. These are generally rectangular, in contrast to the round block signals, and the two aspects are horizontal rather than vertical. There are also rectangular signals at points and crossovers, which show green for the main line and yellow for the branch, in each case with an arrow superimposed. A red indication is given only when the points are changing. There are also various fixed signals to indicate speed limits, etc., and markings by the trackside or on the tunnel walls (a white bar and circle on a dark background) warn of reduced visibility or restricted width.

At certain specially chosen locations in the open air, signal aspects are being renewed using fibre optic lenses. These, although very costly, give greatly improved sighting in conditions of poor visibility.

The maximum speed allowed on the Métro is 70kph, but this is only possible in the outer suburban sections, where stations are not so close together. Otherwise, the speed allowed is shown by illuminated signs, white on a dark background, and applies from speed restriction to speed restriction, or, if it applies first, the next station. Where the speed may be increased between stations, then this is also shown at the appropriate location.

At terminal stations, the signalling is worked by the local signal cabin, often situated on an overbridge with a view of the station. Here, according to the age of the location, a Chef de Manœuvre may have very modern push-button equipment for operating signals and points, or an old style lever frame, some of which are akin to 'beer handles'. Such examples of the latter still exist, but their days are numbered and will be replaced in the near future.

An illuminated diagram of the local area is provided, as well as a visual display unit, which shows the position of all trains bound for that terminus on the line, which greatly assists in the forward planning of departure regulation.

At intermediate reversing points along the line, there are two methods of operation. At selected sites, service reversing is performed automatically by the operation of a single switch in the control centre (PCC). The occupation of track circuits and the passage of trains is all that is needed for this system to operate. At other less important emergency reversing points, large levers by the trackside require manual intervention and operation, but authority to operate them is given by the control room. This system is also provided at the many interconnections between Métro lines.

Automatic Train Operation

The first experiments on the Métro with Automation Train Operation (ATO or Pilotage Automatique) were carried out from 1951 on the shuttle line (the 'Navette'), concurrently with the experiments with pneumatic tyres on rolling stock. Passengers were carried on the single motor coach most weekday afternoons from 13 April 1952 to 31 May 1956, and the system proved to be totally safe and reliable in operation. However, the RATP recognised that there was a difference between testing this system on the quiet backwater of the Navette, and putting it into full operation on a line as busy as line 4. Unfortunately, there was not at that time the finance available to allow a more extensive trial and another decade was to elapse before the idea was revived.

In 1967, line 11 was equipped for ATO and two trains were equipped with the necessary apparatus. Again, there was complete success in operation and all trains were converted by 1969. From then, conversion of the other lines followed, the programme being concluded with line 2 in July 1979. Lines 10, 3bis and 7bis do not have service intervals that are sufficiently short to warrant the expense of conversion to automatic operation and have instead been converted to non-automatic one-person-operation.

The system of ATO used on the Métro is based on an induction cable, carrying current drawn from the signalling system and laid between the running rails to the 'Greek pattern'. The cable has a PVC covering and lies on a wooden surface, which is fixed to the sleepers. Messages transmitted by the cable are picked up by two collectors placed underneath the middle coach. The cable is divided into unequal segments, the length of which is defined by the speed of transmission of information and the speed of the train; the average length of time taken to traverse one section is 0.3 second. The cable carries two programmes, one for acceleration and one for braking. If a train passes through a section more quickly than it should do, the control equipment activates the brakes until the desired speed is reached; if it is going too slowly, it is made to accelerate. The control equipment itself takes up little space and is housed under one of the seats in the middle coach. In the early applications, it operated on the notches of the controller, but now the process is entirely electronic.

In conjunction with the introduction of programmed departures from terminal stations (q.v. below), the clock giving the departure time passes on information to the control equipment, which then requests the departure signal from the driver.

In service, ATO has proved to be very reliable. At stations, trains are brought to a halt within 500mm of the desired stopping point.

The ATO equipment on the Métro may be classified into two categories, which mainly differ by the frequency band of the electronic signals in between track and machine. Thus, there are the low frequency collecting systems in the 3 to 8kHz range, as used on the earliest lines (1, 3 and 4) and the 135kHz collecting systems on lines 2, 5, 6, 7, 8, 9, 11, 12 and 13. This latter system is the most recent and incorporates the latest technological advances, allowing a more flexible operating mode.

Lines were converted to ATO as follows:

September 1967	–	Line 11	June 1976	–	Line 8
February 1971	–	Line 4	April 1977	–	Line 13
February 1972	–	Line 1	July 1977	–	Line 7
July 1973	–	Line 3	December 1977	–	Line 12
February 1975	–	Line 6	April 1978	–	Line 5
May 1975	–	Line 9	July 1979	–	Line 2

When lines were being converted for ATO, the facility for full-speed manual driving was retained, and indeed, it is stipulated that the first train of the day must travel in normal manual mode. Where service intervals are less than two minutes, ATO is obligatory; service intervals in excess of four minutes demand manual driving. Between the two, the driver has a choice. Originally, ATO was obligatory, except for shunting, but following some shunting mishaps due to driver unfamiliarity, the system just described was introduced.

For those lines not equipped for ATO (10, 3bis and 7bis) and subsequently for manual driving on ATO lines, the system of controlled manual operation has been developed (CMC) especially for one-person-operated trains. This consists of a deadman's pedal and a ring around the controller handle, one of which must be operated every 30 seconds. If a driver omits to do so, a bell will sound in the cab, and if that does not have the desired effect in 2 ½ seconds, an emergency brake application follows. Cab signalling repeats the lineside signals, and again, if these are not observed, the brakes will be applied. This information is also transmitted to the control centre, which takes all the necessary steps in dealing with such situations.

All Métro rolling stock has, therefore, been equipped for CMC, as follows:

Line	Line Equipped	Stock Equipped	Completion
1	1983-84	1983-85	June 1985
2	1982-84	1981	February 1984
3	1981	1979-80	September 1981
4	1983-85	1982-84	June 1985
5	1983-84	1982-83	April 1985
6	1982-84	1982-83	April 1984
7	1982	1980-81	November 1982
8	1981	1980-81	May 1982
9	1983-84	1982-84	August 1984
10	1974-75	1975-76	1975-76
11	1981	1980-81	August 1981
12	1983	1983	November 1983
13	1980	1979-80	August 1980

Train Service Control

In former times, when the Métro operated with short trains and short interstation distances, the frequency of trains was comparatively low. However, as traffic has risen, it has been necessary to increase frequencies during busy times, and service regularity has become increasingly sensitive to even slight disturbances.

At the start it was incumbent on the supervising staff distributed over the lines to take appropriate corrective measures in the event of breakdowns. This often led to long, random and imprecise service intervals. Before the advent of the central control room, heavy rush hour traffic and subsequent extended station stops generated late running of services. On line 1, for example, the accumulated late running in the peaks under normal conditions was 22 minutes.

To enable more efficient control of trains, therefore, the RATP has, over a period of time, linked its Métro lines to a central control, or PCC (Poste de Commande Centralisée), where all operations are monitored. Rapid communications are provided in the form of telephone links to key locations, and a two-way high-frequency carrier wave radio between drivers and the PCC. An illuminated diagram for each line is provided, arranged in pairs, one above the other, where train movement can be observed by train numbers and track circuit occupation. In the event of a service disruption, the controllers have every facility to deal with the situation. This may vary from spacing out trains to allow equal but maximum loading, to reversing the service short of a breakdown and operating an emergency timetable. Each diagram has facilities to charge or discharge traction current, or to divide a section. Other facilities provided include signal telephone communications, control of the remaining portillon gates at platform entrances (the high service reliability of recent years, through central control, ATO, programmed departures and reduced station stop times, has made these almost unnecessary), and direct communication with station ticket offices. Although service regulation is carried out by computer, it is possible for manual intervention by the PCC. In either case, a train being held for regulation is indicated to the driver by three flashing white lights in a triangular shape, located adjacent to the station starting signal.

The Métro control centre is at Boulevard Bourdon, and comprises two rooms for the complete Métro network. Line diagrams are arranged in pairs and here line 2 is seen above line 6. The diagram is able to display the position of trains, occupation of track circuits, aspects of controlled signals and the indications of power points. All the facilities for the switching of current are also available on the diagram. The Controller however would normally be seated at a desk containing telephones, train radio and all relevant line information. RATP

The PCC is located in Boulevard Bourdon, almost diagonally opposite the entrance to the closed station of Arsenal on line 5. It is within short walking distance of Bastille (lines 1, 5 and 8), Quai de la Rapée (5) and Sully Morland (7). The first line to be connected to PCC operation was line 1 on 15 June 1967, and immediately the peak accumulated late running on that line diminished from 22 minutes to just 2½ minutes. Other lines were subsequently linked to PCC operation, the last being achieved in 1975. Dates were as follows:

June 1967	–	Line 1	May 1973	–	Line 2
September 1967	–	Line 11	June 1973	–	Line 5
February 1969	–	Line 4	July 1974	–	Line 13
March 1969	–	Line 7	July 1974	–	Line 14*
February 1970	–	Lines 3/3bis	September 1974	–	Line 10
October 1970	–	Line 9	November 1974	–	Line 6
May 1971	–	Line 8	February 1975	–	Line 7bis
September 1971	–	Line 12			

Note* Merged with line 13 on 9 November 1976.

The PCC actually comprises two large circular rooms, interconnected, one with lines 2, 5, 6, 10, 11 and 13, the other containing lines 1, 3/3bis, 4, 7/7bis, 8, 9 and 12.

There are still a number of portillon gates in position on the Métro, but they are now very rarely used. In times past their operation was by the passage of trains but now, if needed, are controlled by the PCC or local station. David Rowe

Programmed Departures

Until a few years ago, the minimum headways during peak hours were not less than 1min 50 sec. In order to reduce these minimum headways on which the carrying capacity of the Métro depends, the RATP came up with an operating principle known as 'Programmed Departures' from terminal stations. Under this system the operating instructions are displayed along successive stations, on a digital clock face telling drivers of each train the 'staggered terminal departure time'. This is the actual time (expressed only in minutes and seconds), less the theoretical travel time between the departure terminal and the considered station. Thus, to follow the timetable, the driver has to leave the station when the time displayed coincides with the terminal departure time. For example, with a train that leaves the terminal at, say 08.05.15, the driver should depart from the stations along the route when the clock displays '05.15'. Each clock also gives the type of running schedule then in operation, which differs during the course of the day. There are four different running times – Heaviest flow peak (marche 'A'), counterflow peak ('B'), midday off-peak ('C') and evening off-peak ('D').

Drivers are kept advised of the permissible dwell time in stations by means of a buzzer, triggered by computer or manually from the PCC. The driver then activates the door closing button which, in turn, activates a pleasant audible sound over the doors, warning passengers of the imminent closing of the doors by a second push on the same button. When a train arrives at a station with a delay exceeding a given threshold, the sound warning by buzzer is given a few seconds in advance of the permissible dwell time to enable the train to absorb its delay a little at a time.

The programmed departures system, first put into use on line 7 in 1969, is now operative on all lines except 10, 11, 3bis and 7bis. By this means, it has been possible to increase the number of trains by shortening the headways (to as little as 1min 35sec), thus raising the line capacity by 15–20%, without changing the signalling system.

Timetables

Train services on the Métro are timetabled to a precision of five seconds. There are three different services provided within the seven-day week: Mondays to Fridays, Saturdays and Sundays. Within these different types of schedules, there are several service level variations, which can be summarised as follows:

On Mondays to Fridays, there are four schedules operated throughout the year. The full service timetable operates from October to April. During May, June and September, a slightly reduced service is provided on most lines, followed by a further reduction for the month of July. The fourth and lowest level of service applies during the month of August, when many Parisians leave the capital for their annual holiday. It should be noted at this stage that, generally, fewer trains operate in the morning peak due to the protracted nature of the morning rush period. In the evening peak, however, where the busy period is more concentrated, the maximum service is operated. For example, the four different service levels for line 5 are as follows; the figures show the number of trains in service for each period and the scheduled service interval:

	Morning Peak		Midday		Evening Peak		Evening Off-peak	
Full Service	40	1 min 50 sec	24	3 min 20 sec	45	1 min 45 sec	10	8 min 15 sec
First Reduction	35	2 min 10 sec	22	3 min 40 sec	40	1 min 55 sec	10	8 min 15 sec
July	29	2 min 40 sec	19	4 min 20 sec	32	2 min 30 sec	10	8 min 15 sec
August	22	3 min 40 sec	15	5 min 0 sec	27	3 min 0 sec	10	8 min 15 sec

Saturdays:	08.00 to 09.00		Morning		Afternoon Busy		Evening Off-peak	
Winter Service	16	5 min 5 sec	17	4 min 45 sec	22	3 min 45 sec	10	8 min 15 sec
Summer Service	14	6 min 0 sec	14	6 min 0 sec	16	5 min 20 sec	10	8 min 15 sec

Sundays:	05.30 to 06.30		Morning		Afternoon Busy		Evening Off-peak	
Winter Service	11	8 min 0 sec	15	5 min 35 sec	17	4 min 45 sec	10	8 min 15 sec
Summer Service	11	8 min 0 sec	12	7 min 15 sec	14	5 min 45 sec	10	8 min 15 sec

Far left **An example of the times displayed, showing each of the four periods of operation. When a train arrives the relevant 'marche' will be illuminated.** Brian Hardy

Left **Every station platform is equipped with facilities for passengers to talk to the Station Supervisor (top yellow section), discharge traction current in an emergency (centre white section) and have access to a fire extinguisher.** Brian Hardy

An elevated section of line 2 looking west from Stalingrad. The ATO equipment is just to the left of the right hand running rail. Note the starting signal which has fibre optic lenses, giving a 'dotted' appearance. To the right of that can be seen three triangular white lights which illuminate to the driver when the service is being regulated. Brian Hardy

Since the last edition of this handbook was published, further help to train drivers using CCTV to perform station duties has seen the adoption of markers added to the monitors to show which part of the train is being viewed, as illustrated here. Brian Hardy

The Paris Métro operates from 05.30 daily, when the first trains depart from the terminal stations. At some former terminal stations, for example, on line 9 at 05.30, trains start from the two termini (Pont de Sèvres and Mairie de Montreuil) as well as from République (both directions), Porte de Saint-Cloud (going east) and Porte de Montreuil (going west). At night, the last trains arrive at the terminal stations at 01.15. Because of the short distances between stations, the complex network of lines, and complex interchange corridors, there are no last train connections between the various Métro lines. In common with other European systems, the Paris Métro is a 365-day-a-year underground railway network – even a good service is provided on Christmas Day with the operation of Sunday schedules from the usual 05.30 to 01.15. The UK public transport operators seem to be something of an exception at Christmas time!

To give an appreciation of the level of Métro services, the trains in service and scheduled frequencies on the Monday to Friday full winter service are given in the following table:

Summary of Monday to Friday Winter Services

Line	No. of Daily Deps	Section	Morning Peak		Midday Off-peak		Evening Peak		Evening Off-peak	
1	360	Château de Vincennes to Grande Arche de La Défense	42	1 min 55 sec	25	3 min 25 sec	47	1 min 45 sec	10	7 min 50 sec
2	345	Nation to Porte Dauphine	35	2 min 00 sec	22	3 min 20 sec	40	1 min 50 sec	9	8 min 15 sec
3	338	Pont de Levallois to Galliéni	32	2 min 10 sec	21	3 min 30 sec	39	1 min 45 sec	9	8 min 30 sec
3b	259	Porte des Lilas to Gambetta	4	3 min 15 sec	3	4 min 15 sec	4	3 min 00 sec	2	8 min 30 sec
4	424	Porte de Clignancourt to Porte d'Orléans	40	1 min 40 sec	23	3 min 00 sec	44	1 min 35 sec	10	7 min 00 sec
5	358	Place d'Italie to Bobigny	40	1 min 50 sec	24	3 min 20 sec	45	1 min 45 sec	10	8 min 15 sec
6	335	Charles de Gaulle-Étoile to Nation	35	2 min 00 sec	20	3 min 45 sec	38	1 min 50 sec	10	7 min 30 sec
7	384	La Courneuve to Maison Blanche Maison Blanche to Ivry/Villejuif	60	{ 1 min 45 sec { 3 min 30 sec	32	{ 3 min 30 sec { 7 min 00 sec	65	{ 1 min 40 sec { 3 min 20 sec	19	{ 6 min 00 sec { 12 min 00 sec
7b	215	Louis Blanc to Pré-Saint-Gervais	6	4 min 10 sec	5	4 min 30 sec	6	4 min 10 sec	3	8 min 45 sec
8	312	Balard to M.A.-les Juilliottes M.A.-les Juilliottes to Créteil	46	{ 2 min 15 sec { 4 min 30 sec	30	{ 3 min 40 sec { 7 min 20 sec	51	{ 2 min 10 sec { *	14	{ 8 min 30 sec { 8 min 30 sec
9	368	Pont de Sèvres to Mairie de Montreuil	55	1 min 50 sec	32	3 min 35 sec	60	1 min 45 sec	16	7 min 30 sec
10	266	Austerlitz to Porte d'Auteuil Porte d'Auteil to Boulogne	20	{ 3 min 15 sec { ‡	17	{ 4 min 05 sec { 4 min 05 sec	23	{ 2 min 50 sec { ‡	8	{ 8 min 45 sec { 8 min 45 sec
11	316	Châtelet to Mairie des Lilas	16	2 min 20 sec	9	4 min 15 sec	18	2 min 05 sec	5	7 min 45 sec
12	305	Porte de la Chapelle to Mairie d'Issy	32	2 min 35 sec	24	3 min 30 sec	34	2 min 20 sec	12	7 min 00 sec
13	394	Châtillon-Montrouge to La Fourche La Fourche to Gabriel Péri La Fourche to Saint-Denis	46	{ 1 min 50 sec { 5 min 30 sec { †	23	{ 3 min 45 sec { 7 min 30 sec { 7 min 30 sec	48	{ 1 min 45 sec { 5 min 15 sec { †	14	{ 6 min 00 sec { 12 min 00 sec { 12 min 00 sec

* Interval is 4 min 20 sec before 17.30, 2 min 10 sec thereafter.

† Two trains in each 5 min 30 sec (morning peak), 5 min 15 sec (evening peak).

‡ Two trains in each 9 min 45 sec (morning peak), 8 min 30 sec (evening peak).

Track

The rails used on the Métro have always been highly standardised. Vignoles rail of a weight of 52kg/m was used on line 1 when it was built. These rails were 15 metres long, but when line 2 was constructed, rails 18 metres long were used and this length has remained standard ever since. The rails are laid on sleepers at the rate of one sleeper every 750mm. They are fastened down with sleeper screws and are joined together with fishplates. The track is embedded in a ballast of crushed stone. On recent extensions, a concrete trackbed with rubber inserts has been used. This latter type of construction is thought to absorb vibration more readily than the traditional permanent way and, as less attention need be paid to levelling, it is easier and quicker to instal.

The Nord-Sud has a more individual elastic approach, probably adopted because of the sharp curvature of line 12. It used bullhead rails, slightly deeper than those of the CMP (165mm as against 150mm) which were supported by chairs incorporating a cushion of linoleum and fixed to the sleepers with a cork insert. The sleepers on the Nord-Sud were spaced at a greater distance apart than on the CMP – 1.40m as against 750mm. Unfortunately the linoleum and cork inserts soon lost their elasticity and disintegrated, causing vertical movements in the track and severe corrugation. Such track had a short life and was quickly replaced by standard construction after the merger with the CMP in 1930.

Welding of running rails was not adopted until 1960, since traditional methods allowed for speedy replacement. However, welding was adopted when line 1 was converted to 'pneu' operation and its advantages were such that it was soon adopted for all lines and by 1980 most track was of welded construction. Only at curves and crossings and on the elevated sections of lines 2 and 6 are traditional methods still used, in the latter case to avoid placing undue stress on the pillars of the viaducts. Rails on curves generally have to be replaced every three years, but elsewhere they normally have a life of 15-20 years.

Because of the normal end-to-end method of operation of most Métro lines, the number of points and crossovers, apart from terminal areas, is relatively limited. Only lines 7, 10 and 13 have junctions (at Maison Blanche, Auteuil and La Fourche respectively), but all of these are arranged to avoid the crossing of lines on the flat, a 'flying junction' arrangement being constructed to avoid the confliction of lines. Many points are normally fixed in the straight position, and often facing points instead of trailing points are used. Points at terminal stations have been electrically controlled since 1911, and many crossovers on the line of route have been similarly equipped since the PCC system of control was introduced from 1967. There remains, however, a number of hand-worked points at locations considered as less important, and at the interline connections. Authority for the use of these points is given by the PCC, although it is necessary for a member of the line staff to be present if used in passenger traffic hours.

The third rail was originally bullhead of 38kg/m but this was very quickly changed to a much heavier Vignoles rail, then again to the present 'T' section rail of 52kg/m. It is placed at a distance of 330mm from the running rail and is fixed by means of porcelain or basalt insulators to every fourth sleeper. Traction current returns via the running rails, which have to be bonded.

It should be noted that the actual track gauge of the Métro is fractionally wider than standard, at 1.44m. In contrast, the spacing between the tracks is only 1.33m, as opposed to main line railways standard of 1.85m.

The track used by rubber-tyred 'pneu' trains consists of two broad 'T' beams of metal, each 300mm wide, placed outside the normal running rails, at a distance from centre to centre of 1.98m. On line 11, much of the original 'pneu' trackwork was originally of tropical hardwood, but this was replaced during track renewal in 1982–83. Reinforced concrete surfaces are sometimes used in stations and, on the elevated sections of line 6, they are ribbed to improve adhesion in wet or frosty weather. Outside the 'T' beams, two lateral bars support the horizontal guide wheels, which also serve as the positive current rails. The ordinary running rails are retained, as are points and crossings, where the beams are interrupted. If a tyre should lose pressure in service (which is a very unusual occurrence) then the train will automatically switch to the use of these rails. The conventional running rails also act for current return and shoes from the train make continuous contact with them, hence them remaining in shiny condition. Conventional rolling stock can therefore operate on 'pneu' lines, but a special lateral current collector shoe has to be fitted.

Electricity Supply and Distribution

It used to be that most of the electric power supplied for Métro operation was provided in the form of high voltage alternating current from three plants and two Électricité de France (EDF) substations located at Saint-Denis, Ivry, Billancourt, Vitry Nord and Arceuil. Three-phase 10,000 volt cables led from the EDF plants to various substations, where the power was stepped down and converted into 600V dc for the Métro, and to 1,500V dc for the Ligne de Sceaux (now RER line B). High voltage cubicles, many of which were located in the substations, make up the grid of the power system.

In 1979 the total revamping of the urban electrical power supply system was completed. High voltage supplied by the EDF from the 63kV grid in the Greater Paris region, to four stations at Monttessuy, Père Lachaise A and B, Lamarck and Denfert, was distributed throughout Paris and from the 225kV grid to three further stations at Père Lachaise C, René Coty and Ney. All these high-voltage stations step down to 15,000 volts for distribution to 138 rectifier substations equipped with medium voltage silicon rectifiers (1,750 to 4,500kW). In addition, given the distance from the high voltage RATP stations, 19 rectifier substations are directly fed from the EDF at 20kV.

The rectifier substations feed the 750 volt and 1,500 volt traction current supplies, so spaced that any one of them can be shut down without detriment, the other surrounding rectifier substations supplying the required replacement power due to their diversity. In each rectifier substation the equipment making up the substation is separated into readily removable, interchangeable and transportable units. Each unit is of standard modules so that in event of a breakdown, it is possible to replace the defective equipment without delay, by means of specially equipped breakdown vehicles.

Power is also distributed to 523 stepdown transformer units (15kV/380–220 volts) feeding power to the electrical installations in tunnels and at stations, as well as to sundry administrative buildings, bus garages and workshops.

The station lighting circuits are fed from transformer substations located in 'power and lighting stations'. For reasons of security there are two entirely separate sources of supply. In the event of failure of the overall RATP power system, standby electric generating sets are remote controlled from the Electrical Control Room (PCE – which actually adjoins the Métro PCC), which clusters together all of the high voltage station controls. In addition, batteries are installed locally in stations to provide spaced-out lighting along the tracks in case of mains power failure.

Substations on the Métro are generally about 3km apart. For ease of identification in the PCC, current sections are named and numbered. If current is required off for any reason, then the tracks in both directions have to be isolated. On the main running lines, it is not possible to isolate just one track, although there is the facility to divide a section to enable an emergency crossover to be used, should it be in the current section with the problem, but away from the actual problem itself. On the other hand, extensive isolation facilities exist at terminal stations, where there are often a number of stabling sidings. Facilities exist on every Métro platform for passengers to discharge traction current. These are contained in a cabinet which has other passenger aids (such as communication with the station supervisor, and a fire extinguisher) and are protected by a glass screen; a pull-ring automatically cuts off the current. These pull-rings are also located in tunnels, spaced at 50 metre intervals.

At night, current is only taken off on the Métro when work in the tunnels or on the track is scheduled. The system must therefore be regarded as 'live' all the time.

Tunnels

Generally in Paris, Métro tunnels have been made as shallow as possible. Only on lines constructed later did these go to any great depth, and this was for the reason of passing under existing lines when they were crossed. New extensions into the suburbs are also built just below the surface.

Some of the Métro was originally built by the 'cut and cover' method, such stations being recognised by their girder roofs. Almost all of the tunnel extensions from the 1970s have been built by this method, where a trench is dug out, the route constructed, and then covered over again. However, much of the original Métro was constructed by the 'Belgian Method'. In this method, a pilot gallery is cut following the line of the upper part of the main tunnel. Shafts are dug to this at intervals for the removal of the spoil. From this gallery, by digging sideways and supporting the earth above by props and wooden planks,

A section of tunnel on line 12 between Solferino and Rue du Bac in May 1990 during the period of time that the track on line 12 was being renewed. Note the 'basket handle' shape of the tunnel, the supports for the original overhead wires and the temporary absence of ATO equipment on the track. Julian Pepinster

space is obtained for building the roof of the tunnel with masonry. Under this roof the gallery can be widened into a covered trench along the line of the tunnel. From this trench, every few metres, side trenches are dug to where the walls are to be built. The walls, also of masonry, are built under the roof, giving a masonry arch tunnel, of 'basket handle' cross section, resting on concrete footings. The whole of the tunnel cross-section is then excavated. The tunnel floor, or invert, of concrete, is next added. The invert is slightly curved in dry ground, or more curved if water is present, in which case it is also waterproofed. Finally, liquid cement is injected behind the masonry work of the tunnel, to fill any voids left by the compression of the soil.

A number of crossings of the River Seine are made in tunnel. These include:

Line 4 between Châtelet and Cité, and between Cité and Saint Michel, both in a double track tunnel formed of a sunken caisson in a trench in the river bed.

Line 10 between Javel and Mirabeau, constructed as previously described.

Line 7 between Sully-Morland and Jussieu is in a double-track shield-driven tube, of cast iron segments, 7.25m internal diameter, as is line 8 between Concorde and Invalides.

Line 12, between Concorde and Assemblée Nationale, is in two single track shield-driven tubes of 5m diameter.

The most recently built crossing under the Seine is on line 13 between Invalides and Champs-Élysées-Clémenceau, opened in 1976.

Depots and Stabling Points

A feature of Paris Métro rolling stock depots is that they are used only for train maintenance and not for stabling trains during slack periods or at weekends. Trains not required for maintenance are stabled 'on the line' at numerous positions, generally at terminal stations on each line. Each line of the Métro has a depot for routine maintenance, and some of these have been specially adapted for repairs and major overhauls. The depots and their locations are as follows:

Line 1   FONTENAY (east of terminus Château de Vincennes)
Line 2   CHARONNE (east of Nation)
Line 3   SAINT FARGEAU (east of Gambetta)
Line 4   SAINT OUEN (north of Porte de Clignancourt)
Line 5   BOBIGNY (between the two Bobigny stations – opened April 1988)
Line 6   PLACE D'ITALIE
Line 7   CHOISY (access from Porte de Choisy)
Line 8   JAVEL (access from Lourmel)
Line 9   BOULOGNE (access from Pont de Sèvres)
Line 10   PORTE D'AUTEUIL
Line 11   MAIRIE DES LILAS (east of station)
Line 12   VAUGIRARD (access from Porte de Versailles)
Line 13   PLEYEL (access from Carrefour Pleyel)

In addition, the depot for engineers' trains is located at VILLETTE, near to Porte de la Villette at the northern part of line 7, with maintenance of engineers' vehicles being undertaken also at Vaugirard depot.

Below Left Depots on the Métro are used mostly for maintenance purposes and not for routine stabling between peak periods. Here, middle motor-car D34 from unit E017 of articulated MA52 stock receives depot attention. Julian Pepinster

Below Right The board showing the stabling positions at Porte des Lilas on line 3bis. Trains from line 3 are also stabled here to beyond the never opened Haxo station. The shorter train stabling positions for line 3bis trains are indicated by the yellow triangle mark in one corner. Brian Hardy

Bottom Right The train position board at Porte Maillot has been amended to show Grande Arche de La Défense instead of Pont de Neuilly, which is now an ordinary through station. The situation is as seen on 8 May 1992. Brian Hardy

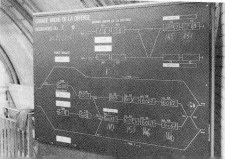

Four of the above depots are in fact located underground, these being Porte d'Auteuil, Javel, Mairie des Lilas and Pleyel. All of the maintenance depots have inspection pits. Most also have lifting facilities and some have travelling cranes to move equipment around the depot area. Three of the depots have been adapted to perform major overhauls. These are at Fontenay (which deals with all 'pneu' stock), Choisy (the first generation of modern steel-wheel-on-steel-rail trains – the MF67), and Saint Ouen (the latest of modern stock – the MF77, and, until recently, the old articulated stock, the MA52). During heavy overhaul, the cars are lifted to allow disassembly and inspection of the major components, such as axles, traction motors, bogies and compressors. There are specialised areas dealing with axle and bogie frame refurbishing, sheet metal work and welding, battery servicing and seat covering repairs. Motor cars undergo a major overhaul at 400,000km intervals, while trailers are overhauled every 500,000km. Painting of the car bodies is not always done to correspond with overhauls and more recently the RATP has had to contend with the menace of graffiti.

Returning now to trains stabled 'on the line', each terminal area has a number of specified locations where it is possible to stable trains. Crews are informed of the train's location by referring to a green chalkboard, which is updated by the terminal station supervisor. Trains are generally identified on these boards by the centre car, and in the train formations they are usually arranged in numerical order of these cars. Identification of the stabling location is by numbers and letters and in places which have more than one arrival and departure platform, these are often used to stable trains, during the day. Often, a serviceable spare train is kept ready to changeover any train that may become defective and will require changing over.

Main overhauls of all rubber-tyred trains are carried out at Fontenay depot. On the right is a motor-car of MP55 stock still in original livery while to its left is a car of MP59 stock in the newer livery. Brian Hardy

The following table lists the maximum number of trains required for service on each line:

Line 1
Grande Arch de La Défense	4
Porte Maillot	12
Château de Vincennes	31
	47

Line 2
Porte Dauphine	6
Nation	34
	40

Line 3
Galliéni	10
Porte des Lilas (3bis)	13
Porte de Champerret	12
Pont de Levallois	4
	39

Line 3bis
Porte des Lilas	4
	4

Line 4
Porte de Clignancourt	28
Porte d'Orléans	16
	44

Line 5
Bobigny	31
Église de Pantin	5
Place d'Italie	9
	45

Line 6
Nation	15
Place d'Italie	8
Kléber	15
	38

Line 7
La Courneuve	13
Porte de la Villette	20
Porte d'Ivry	9
Mairie d'Ivry	10
Villejuif-Louis Aragon	13
	65

Line 7bis
Pré-Saint-Gervais	6
	6

Line 8
Balard	9
Lourmel	4
République	4
Maisons-Alfort-les Juilliottes	15
Créteil-Préfecture	19
	51

Line 9
Pont de Sèvres	10
Porte de Saint-Cloud	26
République	2
Porte de Montreuil	7
Mairie de Montreuil	15
	60

Line 10
Gare d'Austerlitz	8
Porte d'Auteuil	15
	23

Line 11
Châtelet	8
Porte des Lilas	6
Mairie des Lilas	4
	18

Line 12
Porte de la Chapelle	12
Porte de Versailles	10
Mairie d'Issy	12
	34

Line 13
Gabriel Péri	7
Porte de Clichy	3
Saint-Denis-Basilique	3
Carrefour Pleyel	7
Invalides	11
Châtillon-Montrouge	17
	48

There are, in addition, a number of stabling sidings around the Métro system, as listed below, although some of them are used for stabling engineers' trains:

Line 1	*Line 2*	*Line 3*
Porte Maillot	Blanche	Arts et Métiers
	Belleville	

Line 4	*Line 6*	*Line 7*
Etienne Marcel	Bercy	Cadet
Saint Germain des Prés	Edgar Quinet	Pont Neuf

Line 8	*Line 9*	*Line 12*
Concorde	Alma Marceau	Trinité
(bay platform)		Montparnasse-Bienvenüe

Former terminal stations continue to have stabling areas for trains, as follows:

Line 5	*Line 8*	*Line 13*
Porte de Pantin	Charenton-Écoles	Porte de Saint-Ouen
	Porte de Charenton	Porte de Vanves

Terminal Stations
Even from the very beginnings of the Métro, the facilities provided at terminal stations were variable. Now, with 13 main lines and two branches there is even greater variety, which provides much operational interest to the student of underground railways:

1. *Reversing Beyond Station*
Here, there are separate arrival and departure platforms and trains reversing have to proceed to a shunting neck, at which there is a narrow platform walkway (called a 'Trottoir') for drivers to change ends. In quiet periods, it is possible for the train operator to change ends and take the same train on its next journey. During peak periods, a number of shunting operators may be available to speed up operations – necessary when service intervals as frequent as 1min 40sec are being worked.

There are several variations to this method of working at terminal stations. The arrival platform may be served by two tracks, in which case trains may be accepted at intervals which are nearly as short as the time required to empty a train in peak hours. On the other hand, if the departure platform has two tracks (and there are instances where terminal stations have two tracks on arrival and departure), then the interval between departing trains may be shortened, or a spare train may be kept at one platform, ready to leave to fill a gap in the service caused by late running, or to replace a failed train. One track at the terminal station usually has an inspection pit, to allow maintenance staff to examine trains.

The above arrangements apply to: Château de Vincennes and Grande Arche de La Défense (line 1), Galliéni* and Pont de Levallois (line 3), Bobigny-Pablo Picasso* and Place d'Italie (line 5), La Courneuve†, Mairie d'Ivry and Villejuif - Louis Aragon* (line 7), Balard and Créteil-Préfecture†(line 8), Pont de Sèvres* and Mairie de Montreuil (line 9), Gare d'Austerlitz (line 10), Châtelet and Mairie des Lilas* (line 11), Porte de la Chapelle† and Mairie d'Issy (line 12), Châtillon-Montrouge†, Saint-Denis-Basilique* and Gabriel Péri (line 13).

At locations marked (*), it is possible for trains to run direct into the departure platform, or into a middle platform (†), to speed up turn round time during service difficulties, or during certain off-peak periods of operation.

One other station with shunting arrangements, but of an unusual nature, is at Louis Blanc on line 7bis, which offers cross-platform interchange with services on line 7. In fact the station comprises two separate sections – southbound on top of northbound. Trains from Pré-Saint-Gervais enter the southbound platform and a shunt operator takes the train out again, once passengers have alighted, clear of the points which then lead to the northbound, into which platform the incoming operator brings the train.

2. Non-Passenger Loops

In this arrangement, trains detrain in the arrival platform and then proceed empty via a loop to the departure platform. This eliminates the need for drivers to change ends and allows scheduled departures at as little as 1min 35sec intervals to be operated, especially on line 4, the busiest on the Métro. It also allows a number of trains to be in the loop at the same time and this facilitates the regulation of the service, as the interval between planned and possible departure times can be observed and adjusted as necessary.

Locations with this arrangement are Porte Dauphine* (line 2), Porte des Lilas‡(line 3bis), Porte de Clignancourt and Porte d'Orléans‡* (line 4).

At locations marked (*) it is possible to run direct into the departure platform, while at terminal stations marked (‡) there is also a 'Trottoir' provided, which can be used as an alternative to the loop.

3. Passenger Loops

These are perhaps the most interesting of the terminal station arrangements, as far as the enthusiast is concerned, with the warren of tunnels and sidings, and trains weaving in between stabled trains. These exist at Nation (line 2), Charles de Gaulle-Étoile and Nation (line 6), Pré-Saint-Gervais (line 7bis) and Porte d'Auteuil (line 10). Unlike the two previous operations described above, the passenger loops often aggrevate any irregularities in the service.

Interesting operating alternatives are available at the two loops on line 6. At Charles de Gaulle-Étoile, with only one track at the station, separate arrival and departure platforms are provided. However, due to the restricted nature of this arrangement, trains do not take their layover time here – this is done at the next station in the southbound direction, at Kléber, which has two island platforms, one for each direction. It is also possible for a train to reverse at Étoile and travel back on the northbound line, gaining its correct track at Kléber.

The loop at Nation on line 6 is in fact only used in the peaks by departing trains. At other times, when trains are stabled on this loop, reversing service trains can either proceed forward to the 'Trottoir', or reverse at one side of the terminal island platforms.

The stabling area at Porte d'Auteuil on line 10 showing trains of articulated MA52 stock. Beyond the stabled trains is the underground maintenance depot of Auteuil. RATP

4. *Dead-End Terminal Stations*

There are only two terminal stations on the Métro which do not have tracks going beyond the platforms, in either sidings or loops. These are at Gambetta (line 3bis) and Boulogne – Pont de Saint-Cloud (line 10), both being island platforms with a track each side. At the former location, this platform was originally used by trains on line 3 proceeding to Paris, cut short when branch line 3bis was created in 1971 so that the main line 3 could serve the then newly built extension to Galliéni. The present connecting subway between the line 3bis platforms and the new Gambetta station on line 3 (Paris direction) uses the tunnel formerly occupied by the Métro.

Interline Connections

The number of non-passenger connections between Métro lines is numerous and no one Métro line is totally isolated, even though a number of connections may have to be used to reach the ultimate destination. The most frequent use of the connections is made by works trains at night, most of which start their journey in the small hours from the depot near Porte de la Villette on line 7, after the last train has arrived at 01.15. The connections are also used, but to a lesser extent, by stock transfers between lines and for overhauls and maintenance.

The length of the connections, of course, varies with the location, but can be as long as 1.83km between lines 9 and 10 from Porte de Saint-Cloud to Auteuil via the never opened station of Porte Molitor, or as short as the length of a pair of points, such as between lines 5 and 7 side by side at Gare de l'Est. The various line connections are as follows:

Connecting Lines	At/Between
1—6	Charles de Gaulle-Étoile
1—8	Champs-Élysées-Clémenceau (1) and Concorde (8)
1—5	Gare de Lyon (1) and Quai de la Rapée (5)
1—2	Nation
1—6	Nation
2—4—5	Anvers (2) and Gare du Nord (4 and 5)
2—3	Père-Lachaise
2—9	Nation
3—7	Opéra
3—11	Réaumur-Sebastopol (3) and Arts et Métiers (11)
3—5	République
3—3b	Gambetta
3b—7b*	Porte des Lilas (3b) and Place des Fêtes (7b)
3b—7b	Porte des Lilas (3b) and Pré-Saint-Gervais (7b)
4—10	Odéon (4) and Cluny La Sorbonne (10)
4—12	Vavin (4) and Montparnasse-Bienvenüe (12)
4—6	Vavin (4) and Edgar Quinet (6)
5—6—7	Place d'Italie
5—7	Gare de l'Est
5—8	République
6—8*	Daumesnil
6—9†	Trocadéro
7—10	Place Monge (7) and Maubert-Mutualité (10)
7—7b†	Louis Blanc
8—9	République
8—10	La Motte-Picquet
8—13	Invalides
9—10*	Porte de Saint-Cloud (9) and Auteuil (10)
9—10	Michel-Ange-Auteuil
12—13	Montparnasse-Bienvenüe
12—13	Saint-Lazare

Notes: * Used for stabling trains
     † Two separate connections, one in each direction

A typical station ticket office on the Métro at Esplanade de La Défense. Ticket offices not only print and issue tickets but code them as well. Brian Hardy

Fares and Tickets

Until recent times, the fare system on the Métro was relatively straightforward. From the beginning in 1900, a flat fare was used and the original fare of 15 centimes second class remained in force until 17 May 1919. With successive increases, this had reached 1.10 francs by 1938, 10 francs by 1948 and 30 francs by August 1951. Fares were then frozen until 1958, when there was a 50% increase to 45 francs. After the conversion of the currency to new francs in August 1960 another increase brought the fare to 55 centimes, after which there was another period of stability until July 1967 when there was an increase to 1 franc. From 1975 there were frequent increases and a single Métro ticket now costs 6 francs.

Books of tickets have always been available but until 1949, these carried no discount. Over the years the discount has been steadily increased and a book of ten tickets ('carnet') now costs 36.50F, a rebate of about 40%. In practice, most passengers who do not hold a season ticket of some kind use a carnet and relatively few travel on full fare tickets.

First class tickets were available on the Métro from 1900 to the end of July 1991, except between 2 January 1947 and 4 October 1948. While a first class ticket did not bring the passenger much more in the way of comfort, it did buy some extra space in the rush hour! Since 1982, first class applied only between 09.00 and 17.00 and there was little surprise when it was finally abolished. First class fares were generally 50% higher than second class. They are still available on the RER.

Return tickets, usually costing only about 25% more than a single ticket were available in second class from 1900 to 1938; from 1937 to 1938, this facility was extended to first class. The Vichy Government in 1941 introduced a 12 journey weekly ticket, allowing a very considerable reduction on the basic fare and, this has remained available, although in later years it has lost out in popularity to the Carte Orange and Carte Jaune. There have also been social fares, e.g. for large families and for war-wounded, etc.

Until 1951, ordinary single tickets carried the name of the issuing station (first class tickets on the Métro had the station of issue until withdrawn). These were colour coded, the first colours used being pink, grey and green for first class, second class and returns respectively. The colours were changed from time to time and the Nord-Sud used different combinations such as yellow, blue and red with a blue band. To economise on paper, the tickets in the 'carnets' were made available for two journeys from 1943 until 1958. At certain times, the reverse of the tickets was used for publicity or advertisements but since 1973, the reverse had a brown magnetic stripe to adapt to the new system of automatic checking. From 1951 until 1973, second class tickets were yellow, from when all tickets were yellow until 1992 when they changed to jade green, following the adoption of a new house style and logo by the RATP. From 1968, the same tickets were used for the Métro and the bus system.

The Carte Orange
The fare system on the Métro and the RER was revolutionised in 1975 with the introduction of the 'Carte Orange'. For the first time the passenger could obtain a ticket, available on a monthly and annual basis, which was valid on all forms of transport in Paris and the surrounding area. This area was divided into five concentric zones, zone 1 being the area within the City, zone 2 the inner suburbs and so on, working out from the centre. Most of the Métro lies within zone 1, with a few sections being in zone 2 and some later extensions on lines 1, 5, 7, 8 and 13 being in zone 3.

Not even the most enthusiastic advocates of the Carte Orange could have foreseen its success. A weekly version, the 'Carte Jaune' was made available from 1 November 1982. While the bus system was the main beneficiary in terms of increased traffic, the Carte soon accounted for 49% of all journeys made on the Métro and contributed to the increase in traffic on the system in the period after 1975. The principle has been copied on other urban transport systems and was the direct inspiration of the London Transport Travelcard.

On 1 January 1991 the Carte Orange and Carte Jaune was extended to cover the entire Region of Île de France and is now divided into eight zones. This of course made no difference to the Métro, but it was of considerable benefit to users of the outer suburban services of the SNCF. At the same time, the format of the card (but not the 'ticket') was changed – it was reduced in size to harmonise it with similar items available and resembles a credit card. As a protection against forgery, it is now sealed in a plastic cover once it has been completed by the user. An extensive publicity campaign was mounted to promote the new Carte Orange and to make potential users aware of its value. The theme of the campaign was 'uniting' – uniting Île de France, uniting home, school, and office, uniting the various transport networks, uniting people with each other in the fight against pollution and congestion. A minitel service was also introduced to give information about the new ticket.

Passengers who wish an annual ticket make use of the Carte Intégrale, which costs 10.5 times the rate of the monthly coupon for the Carte Orange.

By law, 50% of the cost of commuting may be reclaimed in the areas concerned. Employers usually refuse to refund over the 50% norm for a commuting season ticket, thus reducing car commuting. This considerably reduces the cost of commuting to the employee and makes these tickets excellent value.

Tickets for Visitors
There are two tickets which are likely to be of interest to visitors to Paris. The one-day 'Formule 1' provides a bargain. It is available (in second class on the RER and SNCF) for various combinations of zones up to zone 4 and can also be bought with validity extended for journeys to and from the airports (Orly and Charles de Gaulle) as well as Marne la Vallée – Chessy (Eurodisney).

For those staying three or five days, the ticket to be used is 'Paris Visite', which works on the same principle as the 'Formule 1'. It is valid (in first class on the RER and SNCF) and can be obtained for either zones 1–3 or zones 1–5. This ticket also gives reductions to certain tourist attractions and river services.

Any visitor staying longer than five days should obtain a Carte Jaune or Carte Orange, valid for a week (Monday to Sunday) or a calendar month respectively. It should be noted that, unlike the two tickets just mentioned, this requires a photograph.

All these visitors' tickets mentioned above consist of an identity card and a coupon with magnetic strip, which is used to open the automatic gates on the Métro and RER. On buses the ticket should be shown to the driver but NOT cancelled in the machine.

Ticket Checking

In times past, fare collection on the Métro was a labour intensive operation. Due to the multiplicity of fares (1st and 2nd class tickets, return tickets, tickets extracted from booklets, weekly tickets, reduced fares, etc.), no automatic vending system could be contemplated until recent times. It was necessary to await the progress in electronics to solve the problem posed by such a complex fare structure at reasonable cost.

On the Métro, ticket checking has always been carried out at the start of a journey, supplemented by random checks on trains and in interchange corridors. Until 1973, control was by ticket examiners. Generally female, there were often referred to by the Parisians as 'tricoteuses' (knitters) and they were reputed to be able to examine and punch 30 tickets a minute without dropping a stitch. Fare evasion, therefore, was virtually non-existent under their scrutiny!

The original tripod type AFC gates on the Métro did not prevent the fare evaders jumping over them and subsequently, many have been fitted with 'paddles' to reduce this. This view is at Jaurès on 3 May 1992, which serves lines 2, 5 and 7bis. Note on the left the outward opening exit doors for which tickets are not required.
Brian Hardy

Later installations of AFC equipment have seen anti-fraud gates fitted. It is not possible to jump over these!
David Rowe

The first automatic ticket checking system was installed at the time the first section of the RER line A was opened to the public in 1969 and the RATP subsequently decided to equip the entire Métro system. However, the fact of the urban network being already in operation made it difficult to suddenly install definitive ticket checking machines. Moreover, it was necessary to gradually absorb the excess staff generated by automation. A transition period therefore, saw the turnstiles unlocked by the passengers themselves, by inserting an ordinary ticket in a type of machine that was already in use on the buses. By this means, an entire station could be fitted out without waiting for the design of computerised systems for processing magnetic tickets. Then, first in a few stations commencing on 8 October 1973, these ticket cancelling machines were replaced by magnetic ticket readers linked to a single data processing system, encompassing the entire urban Métro. By October the following year, the urban system had been completely re-equipped with magnetic ticket gates.

Publicity: the Success of 'Le Ticket'
Neither the CMP nor the RATP made much effort to develop a house style for use on posters or in publicity material. The result of this was shown by a survey made in 1973 which revealed that, while most Parisians held a personal view of the buses and the Métro, they were totally vague about the RATP itself. It was decided to remedy this situation, in parallel with the improvements to the Métro system generally, and with the alterations then being made to ticketing.

The first publicity campaigns were purely informative and were linked to developments such as automatic ticketing or the modernisation of stations, and though successful enough did not raise public awareness of the system as a whole, nor did they reach those who were not using public transport. The launch of the 'Carte Orange' was seized upon as an opportunity to promote the use of RATP services, as an alternative to the car and in 1978 this campaign concentrated on the theme of the 'second car'. It depended on rational arguments and eschewed the fantasy of London Transport, which put a tube train into a suburban garage – perhaps for that reason it was unsuccessful. A second campaign associated the users of public transport with trendy activities such as jogging, and was rather better received, but the motorists in general still stayed in their cars.

What was in fact still lacking was a brand image for the RATP and its services, and in 1981 a solution, brilliant in its simplicity, was conceived. The brand image would be the ticket, the ordinary yellow and brown Métro and bus ticket. A pre-test showed that this could go down very well with the public. Starting with the second car campaign the ticket featured in successive campaigns where it was associated with articles such as Levi jeans and Lacoste shirts, the idea being to convey an image of taste and comfort, laced with a dash of snob-appeal. The campaign was backed by a short film 'Ticket Chic, Ticket Choc' which won considerable acclaim in the media, and the music from which became a hit single. Since then the ticket has been the star of many publicity campaigns and has assumed many forms – a violin, a tennis racquet, ballet shoes and other fantasies. Occasionally the images verged on the surreal, as when the ticket became a Star of Bethlehem at Christmas 1982 (presumably wise men travel by the RATP), but there is no doubt that the ticket imprinted the RATP and its facilities firmly on the commercial life of the capital. In 1983 the Poster Museum in Paris ran a special exhibition in honour of the campaign, the publicity for which 'Le Musée à la ticket' won the annual prize for the best poster.

But as successful as 'Le Ticket' was in terms of visual identity (the erstwhile RATP boutique at Châtelet-les-Halles station sold a variety of goods and souvenirs featuring the ticket in one form or another), the RATP wanted to create a totally new visual identity to coincide with a new image. To that end, the new image and new company logo were launched in January 1992. The logo comprises a green circle, representing a 'green' Paris, which is cut by a blue line representing the River Seine, but in the shape of a human face, looking up towards the future, and portrays the RATP's new image of being more welcoming and human. The new logo is now widely used throughout the RATP, on documentation, publicity and rolling stock (a gradual process) and from 21 March 1992, the familiar yellow tickets were ousted by new 'green' tickets bearing the new logo.

CHAPTER SIX
THE FUTURE

The present-day urban geography of the Île-de-France region is the result of plans drawn up in the 1960s, during the first heady expansionist years of the Fifth Republic. These plans led to the creation of the development at La Défense, the expansion of the RER, the creation of five new towns and the construction of the Boulevards Périphériques. While in many ways ahead of their time, the plans of Paul Delouvrier could not have foreseen the growth of population in the Region, now expected to reach 13.1 million by 2015. Nor could the continuing growth of Paris as a centre of employment have been anticipated. The result is that long-distance commuting has increased, that there has been growing disequilibrium between the location of homes and of employment and that inter-suburban journeys, in eight out of ten cases made by car, have become a significant factor in the travel patterns of the Region.

While these problems have been recognised for some time, it was only in July 1989 that the then Prime Minister, Michel Rocard, first indicated that the government intended to take the necessary steps to deal with them. In turn, the State, the Region and the City published in January 1990 a White Paper emphasising the need to invest quickly and decisively in transport infrastructure. These ideas were refined in the discussions leading to the compilation of the next structure plan for the Region ('Schéma Directeur d'Aménagement et d'Urbanisme' or SDAU). The proposals, which will govern planning in the Region for the next twenty five years, are currently being debated.

Few previous plans have placed a comparable emphasis on public transport and the whole scheme is in marked contrast to the market-led approach current in the UK. Such plans do not come cheap and the entire cost has been calculated to be 260 milliard francs at the prices ruling in 1991. But all the authorities concerned are committed to preventing the creation of a barren megalopolis in the Region and at present appear to think that this is a price well worth paying. The plans have many aspects, including the possible creation of a sixth new town at Roissy, the strengthening of the economies of the existing five and the expansion of five towns on the outer border of the Region. Approximately half the expenditure will be on roads, including motorways. But, particularly in the City and in the inner suburbs, the emphasis is on the improvement of public transport. These plans encompass all forms of transport, from waterbuses on the Seine to new lines and stations for TGV-services and, while only those proposals affecting the RATP rail services will be considered in detail here, it is important to remember that these are only part of a very much larger whole.

Extensions and Météor
In 1973, after the completion of the extension of line 3, and while the extensions of lines 8 and 13 were proceeding, an overall plan for future extensions to the Métro was drawn up which, in 1976, was incorporated into the Government's plans for urban development in the Île de France Region. These extensions were intended to satisfy four objectives:
– Improvement in the accessibility of Paris to the inhabitants of the inner suburbs, and, by feeder bus routes to those of the outer suburbs,
– Increasing mobility for those who were not car owners, thus lessening social inequalities,
– Reduction in traffic congestion and its associated nuisances, and
– Improvement in the flow of traffic.
In all, twelve extensions were planned at the time which would have effectively doubled the coverage of the inner suburbs by the Métro. Those already open or under construction have been covered under the appropriate lines, but the actual realisation of all such

extensions depends on various criteria, quite apart from cost. Population and the number of jobs in an area, socio-economic returns, the effect on other forms of transport and on urban development generally are all taken into account by the Regional Council when deciding the order of priority.

However, in January 1992, work began on a brand new line, the first totally new Metro line since the opening of line 14 in 1937. Known as Météor (Métro Est Ouest Rapide or East West Express Métro), it originated in plans to relieve line A of the RER between Gare de Lyon and Auber, but its importance has since increased beyond that and it is now linked to several major developments in the areas of Paris it will serve.

Météor will begin in the 13th district, in the south-eastern part of the city, an area not at present well served by the Métro. The terminus, ZAC de Tolbiac (ZAC is an abbreviation for an Urban Development Zone), will serve a new development and will have interchange with RER line C, whose present station of Boulevard Masséna will be relocated to provide this – all trains on line C will then stop at Masséna. From there it will run via a new station, Dijon (for ZAC de Bercy), to Gare de Lyon where there will be an interchange with line 1 and lines A and D of the RER, as well as other SNCF services. The next station will be Châtelet, where there will be interchange with lines 1, 4, 7 and 11 and RER lines A, B and D. From there, Météor will run to Pyramides, to connect again with line 7, and on to a provisional terminus at Madeleine (lines 8 and 12). Opening of this first stage, 7.2 km long, is planned for 1996.

However, extensions at both northern and southern ends of the line are already planned. From Madeleine the line will be extended via Saint-Lazare and Brochant to pick up the branch of line 13 west of La Fourche and run to Asnières-Gennevilliers (Gabriel Péri) and thence to Port de Gennevilliers. To avoid total saturation of line 13, this extension will open at the same time as the Éole line of the RER (line E) and interchange with that line will be provided.

In the south, Météor will be extended to Maison Blanche by the end of 1998 and to Cité Universitaire and Porte d'Orléans at a later date. When complete, Météor will be 19.6km in route length.

Météor will differ in several important respects from the other lines of the system. Operation will be entirely automatic and trains will not have driving cabs. The platforms will be enclosed from the tracks by glass partitions, with sliding doors to give access to the trains, as on the VAL line in Lille or on the Singapore Metro. The average distance between stations, 2km, will be greater than that on the present lines, (500m – 700m), allowing a service speed of 40km/hour against 25km/hour and this in turn will increase the capacity of the line. When in full operation, with eight coach trains, Météor will be able to carry 40,000 passengers per hour, an increase of 33% over the conventional system. At first, trains will be limited to six coaches. In tunnels a walkway will be provided to allow passengers to evacuate trains easily in an emergency and all stations will be fully accessible to passengers who have problems of mobility or who are encumbered by heavy luggage.

The extent of interchange facilities is noteworthy, all stations on the initial stretch except Dijon having connections with at least one other line, and these opportunities will greatly speed up the journeys of many passengers.

It is expected that in 1996, Météor will carry 96 million passengers, or 8% of the entire traffic of the Métro, and that this figure will rise to 200 million when the line has been opened throughout. Much of this will come from line A of the RER, which should be relieved of about 12,000 passengers per hour over the section Gare de Lyon to Châtelet during the peak period. A more striking improvement in service will occur when Météor is extended over the branch of line 13, at present one of the most overcrowded sections of the Métro, with standing loads in the evening peak of 5 passengers per square metre. Météor will allow a service of 40 trains per hour on the branch in place of the present 12 and in turn this will allow an increase of capacity of 50% on the Saint-Denis section of line 13.

While much of the work will be executed by a tunnelling shield, there will also be a need for traditional methods of construction. To avoid disturbance to street traffic, spoil will be lifted to the surface by a shaft in the Seine at the Pont de Sully and removed by barge.

The initial plans for stations were intended to emphasise the relationship between the Métro and the urban areas above and would have included a viaduct crossing of the Seine and shafts to bring daylight into the heart of a station. Budgetary constraints have meant that such interesting ideas will not be put into effect but nevertheless, the architecture of the stations will represent a complete break with tradition and will be based on the principle that stations are themselves buildings and not simply a collection of corridors. The ticket halls will be wide and will contain not only ticket windows and machines but also telephones and bank cash machines. The floor will be treated as a pavement, as an extension of the street above. Passengers will then proceed to a mezzanine which will lead down to the platforms. These will be embellished with metal arcs, which will contain the access doors to the trains and will be of similar form to the trains. The station at ZAC de Tolbiac will be built in conjunction with redevelopment of the surrounding area and will be of monumental style, with stone pillars and walls of polished concrete, relieved by swathes of red and green. In all stations, the arrangement of light fittings will be carefully studied and the density of light will become stronger the further the passenger descends from street level.

Other Extensions

Apart from Météor, the only other extension of the urban Métro planned for the 1990s is that on line 13 from Saint-Denis-Basilique to Saint-Denis-Université (q.v. line 13, Chapter 2). Other extensions currently under consideration are:
– Line 2 from Porte Dauphine to Suresnes, to interchange with SNCF suburban services and a possible tram link.
– Line 7 from La Courneuve to Aulnay-sous-Bois or Dugny.
– Line 8 from Créteil Préfecture to Parc Régional.
– Line 12 from Mairie d'Issy to an interchange with the proposed Tram Val-de-Seine and RER line C in Issy.
After the year 2000, it is probable that inter-suburban journeys in the inner area will increase greatly over today's figure and it will therefore be necessary to ensure that the proportion of these journeys made by public transport is much higher than the present 14%. The creation of a network of rail links of various kinds – Métro, light rapid transit or VAL – to a density almost equalling that of the present system within Paris, is thought to be the best way of achieving this result. Under this plan, the most likely extensions of the Métro are as follows:
– Line 1 from La Défense to Nanterre-la-Boule.
– Line 4 from Porte d'Orléans to Petit Bagneux.
– Line 10 from Gare d'Austerlitz to Ardoines.
– Line 11 from Mairie des Lilas to Romainville and Rosny-Bois Perrier.
– Line 12 from Porte de la Chapelle to Aubervilliers.
It is planned that these lines would be converted to driverless operation as and when the extensions are built.

In addition to the plans of the RATP, the Region has suggested that the extension of line 10 should incorporate a branch to Champigny-le-Plant, where there would be an interchange with the new RER Éole line and that line 10 should then become a second 'Météor'. The Region would also like to see the construction of a third 'Météor' line from Gare d'Austerlitz and Gare de Lyon to Villetaneuse, north of Saint-Denis, with a branch to Nation – such a line could use the Petite Ceinture within Paris. The proposed extension of line 9 from Mairie de Montreuil to Rosny-sous-Bois is now to be subsumed by the line 11 extension to Rosny-Bois Perrier, while that at the southern end of line 13, mentioned in the first edition of this book, appears to have been dropped from current plans.

There are plans for another extension of line 1 beyond La Défense (in the background) towards Nanterre-la-Boule. The train ascends from the tunnel near Pont de Neuilly and comprises MP59 stock (refurbished and with new RATP logo). Brian Hardy

A model showing how Madeleine station will look when served by the new Météor line. As the line will be completely automatic, platform doors will be fitted at every station, as in Lille. RATP

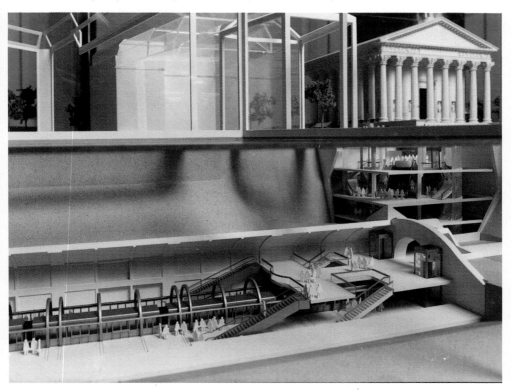

APPENDIX ONE
THE MONTMARTRE FUNICULAR

The hill of Montmartre, to the north of the city of Paris, has for centuries been associated with both religion and holidays. A convent was founded in 1155 – commemorated today by the station Abbesses on line 12 – and in July 1611 it is recorded that Queen Marie de Médici made an excursion to the hill, accompanied by 60,000 Parisians – clearly the problem of crowds is nothing new to the area! The convent was closed down during the Terror in 1794 and in the nineteenth century Montmartre became something of an industrial centre; a photograph of 1869 shows no fewer than 30 mills in operation there and, possibly to serve these, a railway line laid on the side of the hill. Nothing is known about this line and it had disappeared by 1890.

In 1873 construction began of the extraordinary church known as the Basilique du Sacré Coeur (Basilica of the Sacred Heart). Building material was carried up the hill by a wagon running on an inclined plane and pulled by a cable attached to a windlass. This primitive predecessor of the funicular was dismantled after the Basilica was opened in 1891. Intended by its designers and builders as an atonement for the socialism of the Paris Commune of 1871, it soon attracted thousands of visitors, both from among the faithful, who came to pray, and from tourists, who came to marvel at the architecture. Some also came to admire the view over the city from the terrace. But for all those, the flight of 222 steps leading up to the terrace proved to be something of an endurance test and to help them, the City Council, having first considered a four-track railway, decided in 1899 to construct a funicular line between the place Saint-Pierre and the rue Lamarck, adjacent to the Basilica. To avoid having to seek government approval, the line was built on land owned by the City.

On 22 July 1899 a provincial agreement was concluded between the City and the Société nouvelle des établissments Decauville for the construction and operation of the line. Without waiting for the final agreement, this company went ahead with construction of the funicular in the first half of 1900 and the line was opened to the public on 12 July of that year. On 2 August 1901 a second agreement specified that the concession was to run for thirty years and the concessionaire was to pay a rental of 15% of the gross receipts to the City. In turn the City provided water at 30 centimes per ten cubic metres. Fares were fixed at ten centimes for the ascent and five for the descent, but at the time when workmen were going to or returning from work, the fare was five centimes in either direction.

As built the line was a double-track counterbalance funicular, 102.8 metres in length. The difference in height between the stations was 37 metres, giving a ruling gradient of 36%. It was operated by water power, the amount of water to be used being in proportion to the difference between the number of ascending and descending passengers. Between the running rails was a rack rail of the Strub pattern which provided for emergency braking; service braking was operated by a brakesman riding on the open platform of each car. The speed of travel was 1.5 metres per second and the journey time 70 seconds. The two cabins could carry 48 passengers each, in four separate, stepped compartments, as on many Swiss lines, and the platforms of the stations were arranged to correspond.

As there was then no other form of transport in the area, the funicular proved to be very successful and was soon carrying around a million passengers every year.

The concession expired on 22 March 1931 but was briefly extended until November of the same year, when the line was closed for modernisation. A replacement bus service was provided by the STCRP, using small one-person operated single-deckers running on a ten or fifteen minute headway. The fare was now 50 centimes and it was perhaps not surprising that the number of passengers carried soon fell to less than a quarter of a million annually.

In December 1933 it was decided to convert the funicular to electric power and to entrust both the modernisation and subsequent operation to the STCRP. The stations were reconstructed with horizontal platforms and the new cabins, which could carry 50 passengers, had single compartments with flat floors. Longitudinal beams of reinforced concrete replaced the wooden sleepers and the rails were fixed to these along their entire length. A Ward-Leonard electric motor of 75kW provided the motive power and the speed was increased to two metres per second, though the journey time remained at 70 seconds.

The funicular re-opened for traffic on 2 February 1935, running from 06.00 to 21.00, on a frequency varying between two and five minutes. The fare was now that of a one-stage ticket on the bus system. The line then settled down to another period of tranquil existence, passing to the control of the CMP in 1942 and to the RATP on 1 January 1949. It was probably on the former date that operation was transferred from the bus section and entrusted to line 2 of the Métro and since then the fare (for either direction) has been that of the standard single ticket of the Métro. When operation had to be suspended in 1962 to allow modification of the supply system, the RATP took advantage of the closure to replace the cabins. The new cabins had aluminium bodies, with fluorescent lighting and laminate interior panelling combining to give a much brighter appearance; the chassis had rubber suspension. Further modernisation in 1975 included conversion to automatic operation and attendants no longer rode in the cabins. The stations were also improved at that time. During this period the number of passengers carried annually increased gradually to around one and a half million, possibly helped by an extension of service to 00.45.

The years after 1975 saw a spectacular growth of traffic and the numbers carried reached a record 1.9 million in 1985. The growth of traffic continued and 2,350 million journeys were recorded in 1989. These figures were reached despite the introduction by RATP of a midibus service known as Montmartrobus; this is used mainly by local residents, while 79% (1986 figure) of the journeys on the funicular are made by tourists, 45% of these being foreigners. Because of its dependence on this traffic, the funicular has always had a problem of its own particular peaks. These are related to the beginning and end of the tourist day and to services in the Basilica. The highest monthly totals are normally recorded in the month which contains Easter and in August and there can be a difference of as much as 140% between the lowest and highest monthly totals. Formerly two-thirds of all journeys were ascents, but in recent years the difficulties of parking around the Basilica have encouraged coach drivers to pick up their parties at the bottom of the hill and ascents and descents are often almost equal.

Despite this increase in passenger numbers, the funicular was always in deficit, with annual working expenses of 3.3 million francs in the late 1980s, against receipts of 1.5 million francs. Closure of what had now become part of the heritage of Paris, as well as a useful transport amenity, was unthinkable and it was clear that only a more modern and flexible form of operation would both reduce the deficit and cope with the acute congestion which was now often experienced as a result of the increase in traffic. The RATP therefore decided on a second complete modernisation and in April and May 1989 undertook a survey of both users of the line and the local inhabitants, to ascertain the improvements which these would like to see as a result of modernisation. The replies indicated that better designed and more stylish cabins, a complete rebuilding of the stations (the lower was particularly criticised for its draughts), an improved level of service and, among tourists, staff with greater awareness of customer care were required. The funicular was therefore closed completely from 30 September 1990 for total modernisation.

The modernisation was carried out by a partnership between the firms of Schindler and Akros, the latter being responsible for the new cabins. It is a relatively small firm based in Savoy and has become known for its work in advanced technology for funiculars and lifts. In 1988 Akros developed the ATT: Ascenseur Tout Terrain (Lift for all types of land formation). The work on the Montmartre funicular was its first major prestige project in a large city, though the firm has recently supplied lifts to various stations on the Métro, such as Cité and Buttes-Chaumont. The total cost of the modernisation was 60 million francs. The new funicular was inaugurated on 4 October 1991.

The 1964-built aluminium cabins on the Montmartre Funicular were withdrawn in 1991 when the line closed for modernisation, although one has been retained by the RATP for preservation. This 1987 view looks down from the upper station.
Brian Hardy

In its modernised form, the line remains a funicular in name only; its technology is now that of two lifts running on an inclined plane, rather than vertically. The cabins are still pulled by cable, but are totally independent of each other. The departure platform is fitted with a detector which notes the number of passengers as they arrive and, if no cabin is at the platform, arranges for one to move into postition. Within the cabin, a similar detector measures the weight of the passenger load and this is linked to the starting signal. At peak periods this is given when the cabin has reached 80% of its capacity, while at other times the signal is given after five minutes, to avoid any unreasonable long wait. An indicator gives the time before the next departure. Operation can be maintained by a single cabin, but if this has made two successive journeys with 80% of its capacity, the second cabin is automatically brought into service. A similar programme controls such variables as braking, opening and closing of the doors and lighting. Cable speed has been increased to 3.5 metres per second, giving a journey time of 40 seconds. The line can now carry 2,000 passengers per direction per hour, as against 1,000 with the former system.

The Montmartre Funicular avoids the need to climb the many steps up to the Sacre Coeur, but even at the top station, there are still a few more steps to encounter. One of the new cabins is seen departing on its descending journey, with the Sacre Coeur forming the perfect backdrop.
Jeanne Gill

An evening view of the Funicular's lower station, which (along with the upper station) has been rebuilt extensively with glass. One of the new cabins is about to depart. Note that side emergency steps have been constructed in the modernisation.
Brian Hardy

The number of operating staff has been reduced to two, both based in the lower station, where one sells or checks tickets and the other provides information and assistance to passengers. All the nine staff who work on the line have voluntarily followed a course in English.

The new cabins, designed by Roger Tallon, are of a much more rounded and less box-like design than their predecessors. With a capacity of 60 passengers, they are also slightly larger. In the rebuilding of the stations, designed by the architect Francois Deslaugiers, much use has been made of glass and stainless steel and great care had to be taken to ensure that none of the trees around the lower station was sacrificed in the modernisation. Both station platforms have platform doors, synchronised to open and close with the cabins.

Thus modernised, this little line, which carries .01% of the total annual traffic of the RATP, should be well placed to serve both the tourists and the inhabitants of the Butte Montmartre well into its second century.

APPENDIX TWO
THE BOBIGNY AND SAINT-DENIS TRAMWAY

After an absence of some 54 years, trams returned to Paris on 6 July 1992, when the first stage of the tramway between Bobigny and Saint-Denis opened to the public.

Approved in April 1984, the 9.1km route serves the Département of Seine-Saint-Denis in North East Paris in the Île de France. From Bobigny to Saint-Denis, there are 21 purpose-built tram stations, each of which have ticket machines and VDU information as to the location (shown in minutes) of the next two approaching trams. Three stations have interchange with three Métro terminal stations – Bobigny-Pablo Picasso on line 5, La Courneuve-8 Mai 1945 on line 7 and Saint-Denis-Basilique on line 13, and one station has interchange with the SNCF/RER suburban services at Saint-Denis. The route is double-tracked throughout and the rails are standard gauge at 1.435m. There are also a number of emergency crossovers. Much of the route runs exclusively on its own tracks but there are many locations where road traffic crosses the tramway, controlled by traffic lights. In Bobigny, a short section of route is shared with buses while in Saint-Denis some of the route is shared with other traffic generally. Current collection is at 750V d.c. from overhead wire.

The north-east terminus is at Bobigny-Pablo Picasso, adjacent to the Métro and bus station, but the line continues beyond to reach the depot at Bobigny. Opened in 1988 for Métro rolling stock on line 5, it was purpose built to service both the Métro and the tramway. The Métro authority thus maintains the tram fleet, although the tram service is actually operated by the bus division of the RATP. A total of 17 trams (101–117) have been built by GEC Alsthom, with the articulation within them by De Dietrich. Each tram comprises three sections – two end driving motor cars (M1 [facing Bobigny] and M2 [facing Saint-Denis], each 13.05m long) and a short centre section (3.30m long) which carries the centre bogie, making a unit length of 29.40m overall. Inside there are seats for 52 (along with four single tip-up seats by the doors adjacent to the articulation area) and standing space for a further 126 passengers. On each motor car the section of saloon between the door openings and the cab is at a raised level to clear the bogies. The double sliding plug type doors open outwards and slide back against the body, much as on the Métro's MF77 stock. Maximum speed is 70 kph. The exterior livery is mostly silver but with blue, jade green and white lining near floor level, which raises at each end on the higher section above the bogies. The trams are based very closely on those used in Grenoble and they are fully accessible to passengers with mobility problems, having adequate space for wheelchairs.

The first of the 17 trams was delivered on 12 February 1992 and initially some were without RATP logos and vehicle numbers and some had incomplete lower-level lining. Following extensive test running and driver training, the official inauguration took place on 30 June 1992 with the public opening between Bobigny and La Courneuve on 6 July 1992, serving ten stations. The route was completed with the opening on 21 December 1992 of the second stage with eleven more stations, westwards to Saint-Denis.

The first tram leaves Bobigny at 04.52 (06.20 Sundays) and the last at 23.30 (daily). From Saint-Denis the first tram departs at 05.30 (07.30 Sundays) and the last is at 00.08. Advertised service intervals are every 9 minutes (6 minutes peaks) on Mondays to Fridays, 10 minutes on Saturdays and 12 minutes on Sundays. In the late evenings, the intervals reduce to every 20 minutes.

The Bobigny to Saint-Denis Tramway, identified on line diagrams as route T1, is the first of what may be a number of orbital tram routes for Paris in the future. At present, in the south-west of the City, the SNCF suburban line between Issy-Plaine and Puteaux (and with a new section to be built eastwards to La Défense) is planned to become a light rail route, 11.3km long and with 12 stations, for which 18 vehicles will be required. Known as Tram Val de Seine (TVS), opening is currently anticipated for 1995.

Although running mostly on its own reserved track, in Saint-Denis there is street running shared with the local road traffic: a tram is seen approaching the terminus at Saint-Denis, passing over the scissors crossover on this rather wet day on 11 January 1993.

Left **An interior view of a tram on the Bobigny/Saint-Denis Tramway. In the left foreground can be seen the ticket validator (also in the centre). The articulated section can also be seen as well as (in the background) the steps up to the higher front section of the vehicle.** Jeanne Gill

Right **An exterior view of the short centre section of a tram, stabled at Bobigny.** Brian Hardy

PARIS MÉTRO TRAIN FORMATIONS

Train formations are normally listed in the numerical order of the centre (former first class) car. This is also used to identify the location of stabled trains. On most stocks, the number, or part of it, can be found under the driving cab windows. Formations may, from time to time, be changed.

LINE 1 — 52 x 6-car trains type MP59 (Refurbished 1990-1992)

3037	4031	6002	5563	4096	3076
3077	4085	6003	5547	4098	3106
3131	4089	6004	5543	4052	3078
3111	4071	6005	5537	4046	3042
3093	4074	6006	5535	4056	3064
3081	4083	6007	5518	4020	3054
3071	4061	6008	5546	4102	3068
3127	4091	6009	5522	4082	3086
3063	4047	6010	5549	4054	3044
3101	4039	6011	5524	4036	3104
3039	4053	6012	5519	4060	3092
3105	4101	6013	5525	4108	3046
3125	4059	6014	5559	4068	3110
3069	4107	6015	5560	4048	3082
3089	4027	6016	5548	4076	3130
3107	4033	6017	5556	4050	3040
3099	4019	6018	5523	4040	3108
3053	4023	6019	5555	4066	3122
3109	4049	6020	5532	4094	3070
3119	4067	6021	5538	4028	3128
3045	4045	6022	5530	4100	3098
3047	4095	6023	5536	4062	3132
3079	4051	6024	5521	4026	3066
3085	4073	6025	5531	4072	3094
3117	4037	6026	5528	4092	3056
3067	4029	6027	5550	4086	3114
3115	4079	6028	5558	4038	3118
3113	4025	6029	5533	4090	3060
3097	4099	6030	5552	4064	3112
3103	4081	6031	5562	4024	3084
3065	4065	6032	5540	4088	3050
3121	4111	6033	5542	4110	3124
3049	4055	6034	5534	4022	3090
3055	4097	6035	5529	4080	3126
3133	4035	6036	5527	4042	3062
3061	4021	6037	5554	4030	3088
3083	4115	6038	5541	4044	3048
3087	4087	6039	5553	4084	3058
3129	4109	6040	5551	4116	3074
3051	4063	6041	5544	4106	3080
3057	4093	6042	5539	4114	3120
3091	4075	6043	5557	4070	3038
3059	4113	6044	5520	4078	3102
3043	4041	6045	5526	4112	3100
3213	4103	6046	5564	4120	3134
3123	4057	6047	5545	4032	3072
3041	4119	6049	5566	4034	3096
3201	4183	6059	5576	4184	3202
3095	4043	6067	5561	4104	3052
3175	4157	6071	5588	4158	3176
3203	4185	6082	5599	4186	3204
3075	4105	6084	5575	4058	3116

Spare Car:
3137 (Unrefurbished)

Summary:

	M	N	A	B	Total
MP59A	91	90	45	46	272
MP59B	7	8	3	4	22
MP59C	7	6	4	2	19
Total:	105	104	52	52	**313**

LINE 2 — 47 x 5-car trains type MF67E

10301	14301	13301	11301	10302
10303	14302	13302	11302	10304
10305	14303	13303	11303	10306
10307	14304	13304	11304	10308
10309	14305	13305	11305	10355
10311	14306	13306	11306	10312
10315	14308	13308	11308	10316
10317	14309	13309	11309	10318
10319	14310	13310	11310	10320
10321	14328	13311	11311	10322
10323	14312	13312	11312	10324
10325	14313	13313	11313	10326
10327	14314	13314	11314	10328
10329	14315	13315	11315	10330
10331	14316	13316	11316	10332
10333	14317	13317	11317	10414
10335	14318	13318	11318	10336
10337	14319	13319	11319	10338
10339	14320	13320	11320	10340
10341	14321	13321	11321	10342
10349	14325	13325	11325	10350
10351	14326	13326	11326	10352
10353	14327	13327	11327	10354
10357	14329	13329	11329	10358
10359	14330	13330	11330	10360
10361	14331	13331	11331	10362
10363	14332	13332	‡11332	10364
10365	14333	13333	11333	10366
10367	14334	13334	11334	10368
10369	14335	13335	11335	‡10370
10371	14336	13336	11336	10372
10373	14337	13337	11337	10374
10375	14338	13338	11354	10376
10377	14339	13339	11339	10378
10379	14340	13340	11340	10380
10381	14341	13341	11341	10382
10383	14342	13342	11342	10384
10385	14343	13343	11343	10386
10413	14344	13344	11344	10388
10389	14345	13345	11345	10390
10391	14346	13346	11346	10392
10393	14347	13347	11347	10394
10400	14348	13348	11348	10396
10397	14349	13349	11349	10398
10399	14350	13350	11350	10395
10401	14351	13351	11338	10402
10407	14354	13354	11351	10408

Spare cars:
10387
†14311

Summary:

	M	N	A	B	Total
MF67E	95	47	47	48	**237**

Notes:
†Concealed lighting, fans and MI79-type grabstands/perches.
‡Experimental bogies by Creusot Loire.

LINE 3 — 45 x 5-car trains type MF67A-D

10025	*14156	12001	14153	10203
10007	11007	12004	11008	10008
10011	14111	12011	14108	10012
10013	14115	12012	14120	10014
10015	14107	12013	14103	10016
10017	14031	12014	14060	10018
10019	14117	12015	14118	10020
10021	14013	12016	14014	10022
10023	14011	12017	14012	10002
10001	14113	12018	14112	10026
10027	14045	12019	14030	10028
10029	14109	12020	14110	10030
10031	14047	12021	14034	10032
10033	14059	12022	14054	10034
10035	14048	12023	14021	10036
10037	14049	12024	14020	10038
10039	14051	12025	14114	10040
10041	14050	12026	14037	10042
10043	14026	12027	*14157	10044
10045	14127	12028	14128	10046
10047	14039	12029	14038	10048
10049	14043	12030	14042	10050
10219	11210	12043	11214	10220
10091	14017	12051	14044	10092
10093	14135	12052	14136	10094
10095	14155	12053	14032	10096
10097	14139	12054	14140	10098
10099	14105	12055	14106	10100
10101	14143	12056	14144	10102
10103	14061	12057	14036	10104
10105	14063	12058	14062	10106
10107	14151	12059	14152	10108
10109	14071	12060	14070	10110
10111	14083	12061	14082	10112
10113	14075	12062	14074	10114
10115	14079	12063	14078	10116
10117	14035	12064	14154	10118
10119	14087	12065	14086	10120
10121	14089	12066	14088	10122
10123	14097	12067	14096	10124
10125	14101	12068	14102	10126
10127	14099	12069	14098	10128
10129	14104	12070	14100	10130
10131	14145	12071	14146	10132
10133	14015	12072	14016	10134

Spare car:
14158*

Note*
B14156 ex-A13069
B14157 ex-A13067
B14158 ex-A13061

Summary:

	M	NA	N	B	Total
MF67W1	2	1	—	—	3
MF67A1	36	20	—	—	56
MF67A2	—	1	—	—	1
MF67B1	3	—	—	—	3
MF67C1	44	22	—	—	66
MF67C1A	2	1	2	—	5
MF67C2	3	—	2	—	5
MF67D	—	—	—	87	87
Total:	90	45	4	87	**226**

LINE 3bis — 6 x 3-car trains type MF67C-D

10215	14023	10216
10211	14046	10212
10209	14091	10210
10213	14092	10214
10217	14093	10218
10207	14142	10208

LINE 4 — 49 x 6-car trains type MP59

†3231	4213	6001	‡7004	4214	3232
3207	4189	6048	5565	4190	3208
3193	4175	6050	5567	4176	3194
3221	4203	6051	5568	4204	3222
3197	4179	6052	5569	4180	3198
3157	4139	6053	5570	4140	3158
3177	4159	6054	5571	4160	3178
3195	4177	6055	5572	4178	3196
3165	4147	6056	5573	4148	3166
3161	4143	6057	5574	4144	3162
3205	4187	6058	5601	4188	3206
3171	4153	6060	5577	4154	3172
3147	4129	6061	5578	4130	3148
3145	4127	6062	5579	4128	3146
3185	4167	6063	5580	4168	3186
3189	4171	6064	5581	4172	3190
3167	4149	6065	5582	4150	3168
3223	4205	6066	5583	4206	3224
3181	4163	6068	5585	4164	3182
3135	4117	6069	5586	4118	3136
3159	4141	6070	5587	4142	3160
3153	4135	6072	5589	4136	3154
3179	4161	6073	5590	4162	3180
3215	4197	6074	5591	4198	3216
3219	4201	6075	5592	4202	3220
3138	4195	6076	5593	4196	3214
3209	4191	6077	5594	4192	3210
3173	4155	6078	5595	4156	3174
3217	4199	6079	5596	4200	3218
3163	4145	6080	5597	4146	3164
3199	4181	6081	5598	4182	3200
3143	4125	6083	5600	4126	3144
3151	4133	6085	5602	4134	3152
3211	4193	6086	5603	4194	3212
3141	4123	6087	5604	4124	3142
3169	4151	6088	5605	4152	3170
3149	4131	6089	5606	4132	3150
3183	4165	6090	5607	4166	3184
3233	4207	6091	5608	4208	3234
3227	4209	6092	5609	4210	3228
3229	4211	6093	5610	4212	3230
3187	4169	6094	5611	4170	3188
3225	4215	6095	5612	4216	3226
3235	4217	6096	5613	4218	3236
3237	4219	6097	5614	4220	3238
3239	4221	6098	5615	4222	3240
3155	4137	6099	5616	4138	3156
3139	4121	6100	5584	4122	3140
3191	4173	‡7002	‡7047	4174	3192

†Whole train with outside door indicator lights
‡MP73 stock trailer car.

Summary:

	M	N	A	B	Total
MP59A	—	—	1	—	1
MP59B	23	22	10	9	64
MP59C	59	60	27	29	175
MP59D	16	16	10	9	51
MP73A	—	—	—	3	3
Total:	98	98	48	50	**294**

Summary:

	M	B	Total
MF67C2	12	—	12
MF67D	—	6	6
Total:	12	6	**18**

LINE 5 — 2 x 5-car trains type MF67A-D
51 x 5-car trains type MF67F
1 x 4-car train type "BOA"

9123	11055	12086	11230	10024
9042	11169	12111	11179	9136

10501	11501	13501	14501	10502
10503	14502	13502	11502	10504
10505	14303	13503	11503	10506
10507	11504	13504	14504	10508
10509	14505	13505	11505	10510
10511	14506	13506	11506	10512
10513	14507	13507	11507	10514
10530	14508	13508	11508	10516
10517	14509	13509	11509	10518
10519	14510	13510	11510	10520
10521	14511	13511	11511	10522
10523	14512	13512	11512	10524
10525	14513	13513	11513	10526
10527	14514	13514	11514	10528
10529	14515	13515	11515	10603
10531	11516	13516	14516	10532
10533	11517	13517	14517	10534
10535	14518	13518	11518	10536
10537	14519	13519	11519	10538
10539	11520	13520	14520	10540
10541	14521	13521	11521	10542
10543	14522	13522	11522	10544
10545	14523	13523	11523	10546
10547	14524	13524	11524	10548
10549	14525	13525	11525	10550
10551	14526	13526	11526	10552
10553	14527	13527	11527	10554
10555	14528	13528	11528	10556
10557	14529	13529	11529	10558
10559	14530	13530	11530	10560
10561	14531	13531	11531	10562
10563	11532	13532	14532	10564
10565	14533	13533	11533	10566
10567	14534	13534	11534	10568
10569	11535	13535	14535	10570
10571	14536	13536	11536	10572
10573	14537	13537	11537	10574
10575	11538	13538	14538	10576
10577	14539	13539	11539	10578
10579	14540	13540	11540	10580
10581	11541	13541	14541	10582
10583	11542	13542	14542	10584
10585	11543	13543	14543	10586
10587	14544	13544	11544	10588
10589	11545	13545	14545	10590
10591	11546	13546	14546	10592
10593	11547	13547	14547	10594
10595	14548	13548	11548	10596
10597	14549	13549	11549	10598
10599	14550	13550	11550	10600
10601	14551	13551	11551	10602

30411	11552	11553	30412

Spare cars:
10515   10604

Line total:
267 cars (excluding "BOA" unit)

Summary:

	M	N	A	B	S	NA	Total
MF67A2	–	1	–	–	–	–	1
MF67B1	1	–	–	–	–	–	1
MF67C2	–	2	–	–	–	2	4
MF67CX	–	1	–	–	–	–	1
MF67D	–	–	–	–	3	–	3
MF67F	104	51	51	51	–	–	257
Total:	105	55	51	51	3	2	**267**

LINE 6 — 43 x 5-car trains type MP73

3501	7001	6501	4501	3502
3505	7003	6503	4503	3506
3597	7005	6505	4549	3598
3595	7007	6507	4548	3596
3515	7008	6508	4508	3516
3517	7009	6509	4509	3518
3519	7010	6510	4510	3520
3521	7011	6511	4511	3522
3523	7012	6512	4512	3524
3525	7013	6513	4513	3526
3527	7014	6514	4514	3528
3529	7015	6515	4515	3530
3531	7016	6516	4516	3532
3533	7017	6517	4517	3534
3535	7018	6518	4518	3536
3537	7019	6519	4519	3538
3539	7020	6520	4520	3540
3541	7021	6521	4521	3542
3543	7022	6522	4522	3544
3545	7023	6523	4523	3546
3547	7024	6524	4524	3548
3549	7025	6525	4525	3550
3551	7026	6526	4526	3552
3553	7027	6527	4527	3554
3555	7028	6528	4528	3556
3557	7029	6529	4529	3558
3559	7030	6530	4530	3560
3561	7031	6531	4531	3562
3563	7032	6532	4532	3564
3565	7033	6533	4533	3566
3567	7034	6534	4534	3568
3569	7035	6535	4535	3570
3571	7036	6536	4536	3572
3573	7037	6537	4537	3574
3575	7038	6538	4538	3576
3577	7039	6539	4539	3578
3579	7040	6540	4540	3580
3581	7041	6541	4541	3582
3583	7042	6542	4542	3584
3585	7043	6543	4543	3586
3587	7044	6544	4544	3588
3589	7045	6545	4545	3590
3593	7048	6547	4547	3594

Spare cars:
3601   †3602

Note:
†Fitted with prototype bogies for Lyon Metro.

Line total:
217 cars

Summary:

	M	N	A	B	Total
MP73A	87	43	43	43	216
MP73P1	1	–	–	–	1
Total:	88	43	43	43	**217**

LINE 7 — 76 x 5-car trains type MF77

30025	32025	31013	32026	30026	30189	32189	31095	32190	30190
30027	32027	31014	32028	30028	30191	32191	31096	32192	30192
30045	32045	31023	32046	30046	30229	32229	31115	32230	30230
30047	32047	31024	32048	30048	30293	32293	31147	32294	30294
30049	32049	31025	32050	30050	30317	32317	31159	32318	30318
30051	32051	31026	32052	30052	30319	32319	31160	32320	30320
30053	32053	31027	32054	30054	30321	32321	31161	32322	30322
30057	32057	31029	32056	30056	30323	32323	31162	32324	30324
30059	32059	31030	32060	30060	30325	32325	31163	32326	30326
30061	32061	31031	32062	30062	30327	32327	31165	32328	30328
30063	32063	31032	32064	30064	30329	32329	31164	32330	30330
30065	32065	31033	32066	30066	30331	32331	31166	32332	30332
30067	32067	31034	32068	30068	30333	32333	31167	32334	30334
30069	32069	31035	32070	30070	30335	32335	31168	32336	30336
30071	32071	31036	32072	30072	30337	32337	31169	32338	30338
30073	32073	31037	32074	30074	30339	32339	31170	32340	30340
30075	32075	31038	32076	30076	30341	32341	31171	32342	30342
30077	32077	31039	32078	30078	30343	32343	31172	32344	30344
30079	32079	31040	32080	30080	30345	32345	31173	32346	30346
30081	32081	31041	32082	30082	30347	32347	31174	32348	30348
30101	32101	31051	32102	30102	30349	32349	31175	32350	30350
30103	32103	31052	32104	30104	30351	32351	31176	32352	30352
30105	32105	31053	32106	30106	30353	32353	31177	32354	30354
30107	32107	31054	32108	30108	30355	32355	31178	32356	30356
30109	32109	31055	32110	30110	30357	32357	31179	32358	30358
30111	32111	31056	32112	30112	30359	32359	31180	32360	30360
30113	32113	31057	32114	30114	30361	32361	31181	32362	30362
30115	32115	31058	32116	30116	30363	32363	31182	32364	30364
30119	32119	31060	32120	30120	30365	32365	31183	32366	30366
30121	32121	31061	32122	30122	30367	32367	31184	32368	30368
30123	32123	31062	32124	30124	30369	32369	31185	32370	30370
30159	32159	31080	32160	30160	30371	32371	31186	32372	30372
30161	32161	31081	32162	30162	30373	32373	31187	32374	30374
30163	32163	31082	32164	30164					
30165	32165	31083	32166	30166					
30167	32167	31084	32168	30168					
30169	32169	31085	32170	30170					
30171	32171	31086	32172	30172					
30177	32177	31089	32178	30178					
30179	32179	31090	32180	30180					
30181	32181	31091	32182	30182					
30183	32183	31092	32184	30184					
30187	32187	31094	32188	30188					

**Line total:
380 cars**

Summary:

	M	NA	B	Total
MF77	152	76	152	**380**

LINE 7bis — 9 x 4-car trains type MF67E

10313	11307	13307	10314
10343	11322	13322	10344
10345	11323	13323	10346
10347	11324	13324	10348
10334	11328	13328	10356
10403	11352	13352	10404
10405	11353	13353	10406
10409	11355	13355	10410
10411	11356	13356	10412

Spare cars:
14307
14322
14323
14324
14352
14353
14355
14356

**Line total:
44 cars**

Summary:

	M	N	A	B	Total
MF67E	18	9	9	8	**44**

9 x 3-car trains type MF88 (being delivered)

88M001	88B001	88M002	88M011	88B006	88M012
88M003	88B002	88M004	88M013	88B007	88M014
88M005	88B003	88M006	88M015	88B008	88M016
88M007	88B004	88M008	88M017	88B009	88M018
88M009	88B005	88M010			

LINE 8 — 59 x 5-car trains type MF77

30029	32029	31015	32030	30030
30031	32031	31016	32032	30032
30033	32033	31017	32034	30034
30035	32035	31018	32036	30036
30039	32039	31020	32040	30040
30083	32083	31042	32084	30084
30085	32085	31043	32086	30086
30087	32087	31044	32088	30088
30173	32173	31087	32174	30174
30175	32175	31088	32176	30176
30185	32185	31093	32186	30186
30193	32193	31097	32194	30194
30195	32195	31098	32196	30196
30197	32197	31099	32198	30198
30199	32199	31100	32200	30200
30201	32201	31101	32202	30202
30203	32203	31102	32204	30204
30205	32205	31103	32206	30206
30207	32207	31104	32208	30208
30209	32209	31105	32210	30210
30211	32211	31106	32212	30212
30213	32213	31107	32214	30214
30215	32215	31108	32216	30216
30217	32217	31109	32218	30218
30219	32219	31110	32220	30220
30223	32223	31112	32224	30224
30225	32225	31113	32226	30226
30227	32227	31114	32228	30228
30231	32231	31116	32232	30232
30233˙	32233	31117	32234	30234
30235	32235	31118	32236	30236
30237	32237	31119	32238	30238
30239	32239	31120	32240	30240
30241	32241	31121	32242	30242
30243	32243	31122	32244	30244
30245	32245	31123	32246	30246
30247	32247	31124	32248	30248
30249	32249	31125	32250	30250
30251	32251	31126	32252	30252
30253	32253	31127	32254	30254
30255	32255	31128	32256	30256
30257	32257	31129	32258	30258
30259	32259	31130	32260	30260
30261	32261	31131	32262	30262
30263	32263	31132	32264	30264
30265	32265	31133	32266	30266
30267	32267	31134	32268	30268
30269	32269	31135	32270	30270
30271	32271	31136	32272	30272
30273	32273	31137	32274	30274
30275	32275	31138	32276	30276
30277	32277	31139	32278	30278
30279	32279	31140	32280	30280
30281	32281	31141	32282	30282
30283	32283	31142	32284	30284
30285	32285	31143	32286	30286
30287	32287	31144	32288	30288
30289	32289	31145	32290	30290
30291	32291	31146	32292	30292

Summary:

	M	NA	B	Total
MF77	118	59	118	**295**

LINE 9 — 69 x 5-car trains type MF67A-D

10051	11052	13011	14018	10052
10053	14033	13012	11054	10083
10087	14019	13013	11081	10088
10070	14024	13014	11058	10064
10067	11060	13015	14022	10068
10061	14094	13016	11062	10062
10063	14124	13017	11064	10058
10065	14025	13018	11066	10066
10059	11068	13019	14137	10060
10069	11070	13020	14056	10072
10071	14067	13021	11072	10054
10073	14066	13022	11074	10074
10191	11192	13023	14116	10192
10077	14069	13024	11078	10078
10079	14073	13025	11156	10080
10081	11051	13026	14072	10082
10085	14068	13027	11221	10086
10075	11084	13028	14119	10057
10169	14057	13029	11056	10170
10089	14125	13030	11090	10090
10135	14126	13031	11136	10136
10137	14129	13032	11138	10138
10139	14058	13033	11140	10140
10141	14131	13034	11142	10142
10143	14132	13035	11144	10144
10187	14040	13036	11164	10164
10147	14041	13037	11148	10148
10149	14133	13038	11150	10150
10151	14134	13039	11166	10152
10153	14150	13040	11154	10154
10155	14149	13041	11156	10156
10157	14029	13042	11158	10158
10159	14076	13043	11160	10160
10161	14138	13044	11162	10162
10145	14084	13045	11146	10146
10167	14141	13046	11168	10168
10165	14147	13047	11152	10166
10055	11170	13048	14123	10056
10171	14027	13049	11172	10172
10173	14095	13050	11197	10174
10175	14130	13051	11190	10202
10177	14077	13052	11178	10178
10179	14122	13053	11180	10180
10181	14121	13054	11182	10182
10183	14085	13055	11184	10199
10185	14055	13056	11186	10186
10163	14052	13057	11188	10188
10189	14065	13058	11176	10176
10076	14053	13059	11155	10084
10197	14028	13062	11198	10198
10200	14064	13063	11200	10184
10201	14080	13064	11202	10190
10224	14081	13065	11204	10204
10205	14090	13066	11206	10206
10195	14148	13071	11196	10196
10005	*14159	*13073	11006	10006

Note: *B14159 and A13073 were ex-N11005 and NA12003 respectively.

9149	11153	12037	11174	9150
9103	11079	12040	11145	9076
9114	11088	12041	11082	9124
9073	11147	12079	11173	9101
9147	11157	12087	11161	9105
9015	11232	12088	11220	9016
9086	11209	12091	11207	9116
9107	11149	12104	11151	9083
9046	11189	12107	11167	9129
9132	11217	12108	11219	9151
9059	11159	12110	11205	9060
9045	11086	12126	11229	9054
9146	11233	12128	11234	9130

Spare car: 11076

Summary:

	M	N	A	NA	S	B	Total
MF67A2	39	22	—	3	—	—	64
MF67B2	1	1	—	—	—	—	2
MF67C2A	2	1	1	—	—	1	5
MF67C	70	55	—	8	—	—	133
MF67CX	—	4	2	—	—	—	6
MF67D	—	—	55	—	26	55	136
Total:	112	83	56	13	26	56	**346**

LINE 10 — 13 x MA52 (2-unit Articulated trains)
20 x 5-car trains type MF67A-D

Formation of MA52 Units — 1st Class shown † thus

E002:	D03	C02	D04		E022:	D43	C22	D44
E003:	†D05	C03	D06		E023:	†D45	C23	D46
E004:	D07	C04	D08		E024:	D47	C24	D48
E005:	†D09	C05	D10		E025:	†D49	C25	D50
E007:	†D13	C07	D14		E026:	D51	C26	D52
E008:	D15	C08	D16		E028:	D55	C28	D56
E009:	†D17	C09	D18		E029:	†D57	C29	D58
E010:	D19	C10	D20		E030:	D59	C30	D60
E011:	†D21	C11	D22		E031:	†D61	C31	D62
E012:	D23	C12	D24		E032:	D63	C32	D64
E013:	†D25	C13	D26		E033:	†D65	C33	D66
E015:	†D29	C15	D30		E034:	D67	C34	D68
E016:	D31	C16	D32					
E017:	†D33	C17	D34					
E018:	D35	C18	D36					
E021:	†D41	C21	D42					

Note: E015+E016 withdrawn from service (at Porte des Lilas).

LINE 10 FORMATIONS

MA52 STOCK

E003 – E022	
E005 – E012	
E007 – E008	
E009 – E034	
E011 – E004	
E013 – E024	
E017 – E002	
E021 – E026	
E023 – E030	
E025 – E010	
E029 – E028	
E031 – E032	
E033 – E018	

MF67 STOCK

9074	11213	11212	11228	9041
9068	11067	12033	11143	9113
9029	11183	12039	11089	9053
9092	11141	12046	11137	9148
9063	11075	12047	11069	9152
9164	11163	12048	11171	9154
9091	11224	12050	11222	9070
9030	11201	12077	11195	9156
9110	11227	12082	11199	9131
9102	11177	12084	11181	9141
9017	11187	12092	11175	9158
9166	11211	12096	11139	9087
9090	11193	12109	11087	9089
9058	11135	12112	11185	9024
9165	11215	12113	11191	9075
9018	11231	12114	11065	9019
9078	11061	12115	11073	9071
9155	11077	12122	11057	9081
9088	11083	12124	11085	9072
9033	11071	12125	11223	9034

Line total:
26 units MA52
100 cars MF67

MF67 Stock Summary:

	N	NA	S	Total
MF67A2	13	6	–	19
MF67C2	26	10	–	36
MF67CX	2	3	–	5
MF67D	–	–	40	40
Total:	41	19	40	**100**

LINE 11 — 16 x 4-car trains type MP55
7 x 4-car trains type MP73

MP55 STOCK

3002	5501	4005	3020
3035	5502	4004	3017
3008	5503	4011	3033
3026	5504	4012	3011
3003	5505	4017	3007
3021	5506	4018	3013
3032	5507	4013	3016
3029	5508	4002	3023
3030	5509	4009	3009
3014	5510	4015	3036
3010	5511	4008	3022
3018	5512	4007	3001
3027	5513	4016	3025
3012	5515	4006	3034
3031	5516	4010	3005
3006	5517	4003	3004

MP73 STOCK

3503	6502	4502	3504
3511	6506	4506	3512
3591	6546	4546	3592
3513	6548	4507	3514
3509	6549	4505	3510
3507	7049	4504	3508
3599	7006	7050	3600

Summary:

	M	N	A	B	Total
MP55A	18	9	10	–	37
MP55B	14	7	6	–	27
MP73A	12	6	5	2	25
MP73P2	–	–	–	1	1
MP86	2	–	–	–	2
Total:	46	22	21	3	**92**

LINE 12 — 43 x 5-car trains type MF67A-D

9100	11027	12031	11020	9057
9061	11092	12032	11037	9095
9021	11112	12034	11115	9020
9112	11025	12035	11029	9119
9118	11122	12036	11111	9108
9035	11049	12038	11128	9109
9121	11018	12042	11028	9038
9140	11030	12044	11091	9120
9043	11165	12045	11063	9085
9145	11013	12049	11110	9077
9051	11002	12073	11105	9065
9157	11203	12074	11053	9056
9162	11046	12075	11012	9044
9080	11050	12076	11117	9050
9115	11014	12078	11017	9117
9144	11019	12081	11033	9143
9036	11021	12083	11042	9062
9097	11093	12085	11130	9093
9122	11016	12089	11041	9134
9127	11022	12090	11109	9128
9084	11094	12093	11073	9104
9142	11031	12094	11106	9082
9125	11126	12095	11043	9049
9031	11100	12097	11099	9094
9032	11034	12098	11114	9066
9026	11001	12099	11040	9160
9111	11035	12100	11044	9012
9022	11208	12101	11108	9039
9013	11102	12102	11104	9052
9079	11048	12103	11113	9023
9138	11032	12105	11026	9163
9069	11119	12106	11039	9098
9048	11118	12116	11125	9047
9126	11103	12117	11116	9014
9064	11098	12118	11120	9135
9137	11096	12120	11095	9037
9028	11047	12121	11107	9153
9139	11036	12122	11045	9027
9096	11124	12127	11129	9106
9040	11015	12129	11011	9055
9025	11101	12130	11059	9133
9159	11038	12131	11216	9099
9067	11123	12132	11024	9011

Spare cars:
9161
11097   11127   12080

Line total:
219 cars

Summary:

	N	NA	S	Total
MF67W1	2	–	–	2
MF67A1	40	–	–	40
MF67A2	3	10	–	13
MF67C1	39	4	–	43
MF67C2	4	26	–	30
MF67CX	–	4	–	4
MD67D	–	–	87	87
Total:	88	44	87	**219**

LINE 13 — 60 x 5-car trains type MF77

30001	32001	31001	32002	30002
30010	32006	31003	32005	30006
30007	32007	31004	32008	30008
30009	32009	31005	32010	30005
30011	32011	31006	32012	30012
30013	32014	31007	32013	30014
30015	32016	31008	32015	30016
30017	32017	31009	32018	30018
30019	32020	31010	32019	30020
30021	32021	31011	32022	30022
30023	32024	31012	32023	30024
30037	32037	31019	32038	30038
30041	32041	31021	32042	30042
30043	32043	31022	32044	30044
30055	32056	31028	32055	30056
30089	32089	31045	32090	30090
30091	32091	31046	32092	30092
30093	32093	31047	32094	30094
30095	32095	31048	32096	30096
30097	32097	31049	32098	30098
30099	32099	31050	32100	30100
30117	32117	31059	32118	30118
†30153	32125	31063	32126	30126
30127	32127	31064	32128	30128
30129	32129	31065	32130	30130
30131	32131	31066	32132	30132
30133	32133	31067	32134	30134
30135	32135	31068	32136	30136
30139	32139	31070	32140	30140
30141	32141	31071	32142	30142
30143	32143	31072	32144	30144
30145	32145	31073	32146	30146
30147	32147	31074	32148	30148
30149	32149	31075	32150	30150
30151	32151	31076	32152	30152
‡30137	32137	31077	32138	30138
30155	32155	31078	32156	30156
†30157	32157	31079	32158	30158
30221	32221	31111	32222	30222
30295	32295	31148	32296	30296
30297	32297	31149	32298	30298
30299	32299	31150	32300	30300
30301	32301	31151	32302	30302
30303	32303	31152	32304	30304
30305	32305	31153	32306	30306
30307	32307	31154	32308	30308
30309	32309	31155	32310	30310
30311	32311	31156	32312	30312
30313	32313	31157	32314	30314
30315	32315	31158	32316	30316
30375	32375	31188	32376	30376
30377	32377	31189	32378	30378
30379	32379	31190	32380	30380
30381	32381	31191	32382	30382
30383	32383	31192	32384	30384
30385	32385	31193	32386	30386
30387	32387	31194	32388	30388
30389	32389	31195	32390	30390
30391	32391	31196	32392	30392
30393	32393	31197	32394	30394

Spare Cars:
30125 Asynchronous motors
               experiments
31069   32153

Notes:
†Fitted with magnetic track brakes
‡Five-car set fitted with white door push-
buttons

Line total:
303 cars

Summary:

	M	NA	B	Total
MF77	121	61	121	**303**

MF67 STOCK SUMMARY

The MF67 stock story is complex. The following may be useful for line allocation purposes:

Type	Line	M	N	NA	B	A	S	Grand Totals	
W1	3	2	—	1	—	—	—	3	**6**
	12	—	2	—	—	—	—	2	
	CI/GA	—	—	—	1	—	—	1	
W2	CI/GA	2	2	1	1	—	—	6	**6**
A1	3	36	—	20	—	—	—	56	**96**
	12	—	40	—	—	—	—	40	
A2	3	—	—	1	—	—	—	1	**98**
	5	—	1	—	—	—	—	1	
	9	39	22	3	—	—	—	64	
	10	—	13	6	—	—	—	19	
	12	—	3	10	—	—	—	13	
B1	3	3	—	—	—	—	—	3	**4**
	5	1	—	—	—	—	—	1	
B2	9	1	1	—	—	—	—	2	**2**
C1	3	44	—	22	—	—	—	66	**110**
	12	—	39	4	—	—	—	43	
	CI/GA	—	1	—	—	—	—	1	
C1A	3	2	2	1	—	—	—	5	**5**
C2	3	3	2	—	—	—	—	5	**228**
	3bis	12	—	—	—	—	—	12	
	5	—	2	2	—	—	—	4	
	9	70	55	8	—	—	—	133	
	10	—	26	10	—	—	—	36	
	12	—	4	26	—	—	—	30	
	CI/GA	6	2	—	—	—	—	8	
C2A	9	2	1	—	1	1	—	5	**5**
CS	CI/GA	2	1	1	—	—	—	4	**4**
CX	5	—	1	—	—	—	—	1	**16**
	9	—	4	2	—	—	—	6	
	10	—	2	3	—	—	—	5	
	12	—	—	4	—	—	—	4	
D	3	—	—	—	87	—	—	87	**363**
	3bis	—	—	—	6	—	—	6	
	5	—	—	—	—	—	3	3	
	9	—	—	—	55	55	26	136	
	10	—	—	—	—	—	40	40	
	12	—	—	—	—	—	87	87	
	CI/GA	—	—	—	—	4	—	4	
E	2	95	47	—	48	47	—	237	**282**
	7bis	18	9	—	8	9	—	44	
	CI/GA	1	—	—	—	—	—	1	
F	5	104	51	—	51	51	—	257	**257**
Totals:		443	333	125	258	167	156	1482	**1482**

NOTE

Various cars are in store or retained for instructional purposes. These are:

MP55 – M3024, N4001.

MP73 – N4550, B7046.

MF67 – M10003, M10004, M10193, M10194, M10221, M10222, M10223, M10225, M10226, M10227, M10310.
N11003, N11004, N11121, N11194, N11218, N11225.
NA12002, NA12119.
A13060, A13068, A13070, A13072.
B14001, B14002.

MF77 – M30003, M30004, NA31002, B32003, B32004.

ABBREVIATIONS USED:

Companies/Organisations

AMTUIR	Association pour le Musée des Transports Urbains, Interurbains et Ruraux
CMP	Compagnie de Chemin de Fer Métropolitain de Paris
EDF	Electricité de France
NS (or Nord-Sud)	Société du Chemin de Fer Électrique Souterrain Nord-Sud de Paris
ORTP	Office Régional des Transports Parisiens
RATP	Régie Autonome des Transports Parisiens
RER	Réseau Express Régional
SNCF	Société Nationale des Chemins de Fer Français
STCRP	Société des Transports en Commun de la Région Parisienne
STP	Syndicat des Transports Parisiens

Rolling Stock/Equipment Manufacturers

Alsthom	Société Alsthom-Atlantique – now GEC Alsthom
ANF	Ateliers du Nord de la France à Blanc Misseron
BL	Brissonneau et Lotz
CAFL	Compagnie des Acieries et Forges de la Loire
CEM	Compagnie Electro-Mécanique
CGT	Compagnie Générale de Traction
CIMT	Compagnie Industrielle de Matériel de Transport
Creusot Loire	Société Creusot Loire
Düwag	Düsseldorfer Waggonfabrik
JH	Jeumont-Heidmann
Jeumont	Société Jeumont-Schneider
MTE	Société Matériel Traction Électrique
RNUR	Régie Nationale des Usines Renault
SFB	Société Franco Belge, subsequently Société Ferroviaire de Valenciennes (SOFERVAL)
TCO	Société de Traction CEM Oerlikon

Equipment/Systems

AIMT	Automobilisation Intégrale du Mouvement des Trains
ATO	Automatic Train Operation (English version). French equivalent – Pilotage Automatique
CMC	Conduite Manuelle Contrôlée
PCC	Poste de Commande Centralisée
PCE	Poste de Commande d'Energie

Rolling Stock Types

MA	Matériel Articulé
MF	Matériel Fer
MP	Matériel Pneu

Rolling Stock Vehicle Types

M	Driving Motor car 2nd class (Motrice avec loge, deuxième classe)
Bb	Second class trailer (Remorque deuxième classe) – Sprague & Nord-Sud stock only
Ab	First class trailer (Remorque première classe) – Sprague & Nord-Sud stock only
B	Second class trailer (Remorque deuxième classe)
A	First class trailer (Remorque première classe) – now second class
AB	Composite trailer (Remorque mixte) – now second class
N	Non-driving motor car, 2nd class (Motrice sans loge, deuxième classe)
NA	Non-Driving motor car, 1st class (Motrice sans loge, première classe) – now second class
S	Driving trailer, 2nd class (Remorque avec loge de conduite, deuxième classe)
Sp	Driving trailer, 2nd class with emergency-only driving desk
T	Works train driving motor car (Tracteur)
TA	Depot shunting driving motor Car (Tracteur d'Atelier)
V	Miscellaneous vehicles (Véhicule auxiliaire)
VX	Special miscellaneous vehicle (Véhicule Spéciaux)
TMA	Battery Locomotive (Tracteur à Marche Autonome)
E	Unit (Elément)

THE FOLLOWING PUBLICATIONS WERE USEFUL IN THE COMPILATION OF THIS HANDBOOK:
ON RAILS UNDER PARIS (B. J. Prigmore, LRTL 1974).
NOTRE METRO (J. Robert, 1983).
LA VIE DU RAIL (various issues)
HISTOIRE DE LA RATP (M. Margairaz, 1989)

ENTRE LES LIGNES
RAILWAY GAZETTE INTERNATIONAL
Numerous RATP documents.
LE METRO DE PARIS (A. Bindi, D. Lefeuvre, 1990)